Jewish Literature: A Very Short Introduction

VERY SHORT INTRODUCTIONS are for anyone wanting a stimulating and accessible way into a new subject. They are written by experts, and have been translated into more than 45 different languages.

The series began in 1995, and now covers a wide variety of topics in every discipline. The VSI library currently contains over 650 volumes—a Very Short Introduction to everything from Psychology and Philosophy of Science to American History and Relativity—and continues to grow in every subject area.

Very Short Introductions available now:

ABOLITIONISM Richard S. Newman
THE ABRAHAMIC RELIGIONS
    Charles L. Cohen
ACCOUNTING Christopher Nobes
ADOLESCENCE Peter K. Smith
ADVERTISING Winston Fletcher
AERIAL WARFARE Frank Ledwidge
AESTHETICS Bence Nanay
AFRICAN AMERICAN RELIGION
    Eddie S. Glaude Jr.
AFRICAN HISTORY John Parker and
    Richard Rathbone
AFRICAN POLITICS Ian Taylor
AFRICAN RELIGIONS Jacob K. Olupona
AGEING Nancy A. Pachana
AGNOSTICISM Robin Le Poidevin
AGRICULTURE Paul Brassley and
    Richard Soffe
ALEXANDER THE GREAT
    Hugh Bowden
ALGEBRA Peter M. Higgins
AMERICAN BUSINESS
    HISTORY Walter A. Friedman
AMERICAN CULTURAL
    HISTORY Eric Avila
AMERICAN FOREIGN
    RELATIONS Andrew Preston
AMERICAN HISTORY Paul S. Boyer
AMERICAN IMMIGRATION
    David A. Gerber
AMERICAN LEGAL
    HISTORY G. Edward White
AMERICAN MILITARY HISTORY
    Joseph T. Glatthaar

AMERICAN NAVAL HISTORY
    Craig L. Symonds
AMERICAN POLITICAL
    HISTORY Donald Critchlow
AMERICAN POLITICAL PARTIES
    AND ELECTIONS L. Sandy Maisel
AMERICAN POLITICS
    Richard M. Valelly
THE AMERICAN PRESIDENCY
    Charles O. Jones
THE AMERICAN
    REVOLUTION Robert J. Allison
AMERICAN SLAVERY
    Heather Andrea Williams
THE AMERICAN SOUTH
    Charles Reagan Wilson
THE AMERICAN WEST Stephen Aron
AMERICAN WOMEN'S
    HISTORY Susan Ware
AMPHIBIANS T. S. Kemp
ANAESTHESIA Aidan O'Donnell
ANALYTIC PHILOSOPHY
    Michael Beaney
ANARCHISM Colin Ward
ANCIENT ASSYRIA Karen Radner
ANCIENT EGYPT Ian Shaw
ANCIENT EGYPTIAN ART AND
    ARCHITECTURE Christina Riggs
ANCIENT GREECE Paul Cartledge
THE ANCIENT NEAR EAST
    Amanda H. Podany
ANCIENT PHILOSOPHY Julia Annas
ANCIENT WARFARE Harry Sidebottom
ANGELS David Albert Jones

Available soon:

For more information visit our website

www.oup.com/vsi/

Ilan Stavans

JEWISH
LITERATURE

A Very Short Introduction

OXFORD
UNIVERSITY PRESS

OXFORD

UNIVERSITY PRESS

Oxford University Press is a department of the University of Oxford.
It furthers the University's objective of excellence in research, scholarship,
and education by publishing worldwide. Oxford is a registered trade mark of
Oxford University Press in the UK and certain other countries.

Published in the United States of America by Oxford University Press
198 Madison Avenue, New York, NY 10016, United States of America.

© Oxford University Press 2021

Library of Congress Cataloging-in-Publication Data

Names: Stavans, Ilan, author.
Title: Jewish literature : a very short introduction / Ilan Stavans.
Description: New York, NY : Oxford University Press, [2021]
Identifiers: LCCN 2021001130 (print) | LCCN 2021001131 (ebook) |
ISBN 9780190076979 (paperback) | ISBN 9780190077006 (ebook) |
ISBN 9780190076993 (epub) | ISBN 9780190076986 (ebook other)
Subjects: LCSH: Jewish literature—History and criticism. | Judaism and literature.
Classification: LCC PN842 .S76 2021 (print) | LCC PN842 (ebook) |
DDC 809/.88924—dc23
LC record available at https://lccn.loc.gov/2021001130
LC ebook record available at https://lccn.loc.gov/2021001131

Printed by Integrated Books International, United States of America
on acid-free paper

To Susan Miron

Contents

List of illustrations

Acknowledgments

Reading is thinking, alone and with others; it is a profusely intimate act yet also a social endeavor. If I pride myself on anything, it is on having a career as a reader.

My first attempt at appraising Jewish literature—its interwoven symbols, motifs, and themes—was the introduction to *The Oxford Book of Jewish Stories* (1998). I had eighteen pages to make my case, so I quickly learned that any précis that aspires to be short must, by necessity, make concessions. While painful, the fact that my reflections anteceded a compendium of what I deemed to be the best Jewish stories since the Haskalah—as the Jewish Enlightenment, roughly from the 1770s to the 1880s, is known in Hebrew (the word literally means "erudition")—made the effort thrilling. Since then, I have edited a handful of similar omnibuses, including *The Schocken Book of Modern Sephardic Literature* (2005), *Oy, Caramba!: An Anthology of Jewish Stories from Latin America* (2016), and *How Yiddish Changed America and How America Changed Yiddish* (2020), each preceded by another maddeningly brief introduction, which, I confess, is the raison d'être I delve into projects of this nature. I am interested in movable libraries—my definition of an anthology: how they broaden and condense traditions, how they invite readers to build bridges across authors, themes, and styles. I have also ruminated on Jewish literature, its substance and edges, in three collections of essays: *The Inveterate Dreamer* (2001), *Singer's Typewriter and Mine* (2012), and *On Self-Translation* (2018).

I appreciate the invitation of editors to set my mind in motion in these efforts. Particularly for this volume, I thank a number of colleagues and lifelong friends from whose nurturing thoughts I have learned enormously: Ángel Sáenz-Badillos, Jonathan Brendt, Marcelo Brodsky, Jules Chametzky, Mindl Cohen, Jeremy A. Dauber, Michael DiRuggiero, Ariel Dorfman, Lawrence Douglas, John Felstiner, Ruth Fine, Tamar Goldschmidt, Hillel Halkin, Katherine Hellerstein, Annette Hochstein, Ben Kaplan, Michael Kazin, Steven G. Kellman, Arthur Kiron, Josh Lambert, Aaron Lansky, David Mazower, Dan Miron, Diego Moldes González, David N. Myers, Anita Norich, Eliezer Nowodworski, Cynthia Ozick, Hannah Pollin-Galay, Raanan Rein, Jonathan Rosen, David G. Roskies, Rachel Rubinstein, Stephen A. Sadow, Howard Schwartz, Rosalie Sitman, Neal Sokol, Werner Sollors, Chava Turniansky, Michael Walzer, Matthew Warshawsky, Hana Wirth-Nesher, Ruth R. Wisse, James E. Young, and Suzanne Zepp. Gracias also to Nancy Toff at Oxford University Press for her advice, guidance, and encouragement in the conception of this book. Her assistant, Brent Matheny, was with me in the early stages of the editorial process. The expert copyediting was done by Deva Thomas. My assistant at Amherst College, Ella Rose, was helpful in all book matters.

I write this these lines at a time of global quarantine, as the COVID-19 virus continues to mercilessly jump from one corner of the planet to another, causing havoc. The number of deaths is staggering. It is a sobering period, prone to introspection. Jews are well tuned to survive such conditions, having learned, time and again, how to cope with the apocalypse. Rereading the Jewish classics has been medicinal to me; as Spanish golden age poet Francisco de Quevedo put it, "Escucho con mis ojos a los muertos"—it has allowed me to listen to the dead through my eyes.

Introduction: People of the Book

In a lecture titled "The Argentine Writer and Tradition," delivered in Buenos Aires in 1951, Jorge Luis Borges, the author of a number of stories on Jewish themes, including "Death and the Compass," "Emma Zunz," and "The Secret Miracle," argues, insightfully, that Argentine writers do not need to restrict themselves to local themes: tango, gauchos, *maté*, and so on. Instead, he states, "I believe our tradition is the entire Western culture, and I also believe we have a right to that tradition, equal to that of any other citizen in any Western nation."

In other words, nationalism is a narrow proposition; its counterpart, cosmopolitanism, is a far better option. Borges then adds, "I remember here an essay by Thorstein Veblen, a United States sociologist, about the preeminence of the Jews in Western culture. He asks if this preeminence is due to an innate superiority of the Jews and he answers no; he says they distinguish themselves in Western culture because they act in that culture and at the same time do not feel tied to it by any particular devotion; that's why, he says, 'a Jew vis-à-vis a non-Jew will always find it easier to innovate in Western culture.'"

The claim Borges takes from Veblen to emphasize is a feature of Jewish literature: its aterritoriality. Literary critic George Steiner, an assiduous Borges reader, preferred the term *extraterritorial*.

The difference is nuanced: aterritorial means outside a territory; extraterritorial means beyond it. Either way, the terms points to the outsiderness of Jews during their diasporic journey. Unlike, say, Argentine, French, Egyptian, or any other national literature, the one produced by Jews has no fixed address. That is because it does not have a specific geographic center; it might pop up anywhere in the globe, as long as suitable circumstances make it possible for it to thrive. This is not to say that Jews are not grounded in history. Quite the contrary: Jewish life, like anyone else's, inevitably responds at the local level to concrete elements. Yet Jews tend to have a view of history that supersedes whatever homegrown defines them, seeing themselves as travelers across time and space.

The focus in this volume is modern Jewish literature in the broadest sense. I am interested in the ways it mutates while remaining the same. Made of bursts of consent and dissent, this literature is not concerned with divine revelation, like the Torah and Talmud, but with the rowdy display of human frailties. It springs from feeling ambivalent in terms of belonging. It is also marked by ceaseless migration. All this could spell disaster. Yet Jews have turned these elements into a recipe for success. They have produced a stunning number of masterpieces, constantly redefining what we mean by literature. Indeed, one barometer to measure not only its health but also its diversity is the sheer number of recipients of the Nobel Prize for Literature since the award was established in Stockholm in 1895: more than a dozen, including Shmuel Yosef Agnon writing in Hebrew (1966), Saul Bellow in English (1976), Isaac Bashevis Singer in Yiddish (1978), Elias Canetti in German (1981), Joseph Brodsky in Russian (1987), Imre Kertész in Hungarian (2002), Patrick Modiano in French (2014), and Bob Dylan (2017) and Louise Glück (2020) in English.

With these many habitats, it is not surprising that Jewish literature might seem rowdy, amorphous, even unstable. It is thus important to ask, at the outset, two notoriously difficult questions: first, what is literature, and second, what makes this particular one Jewish? The answer to the first is nebulous. Jewish writers write stories, essays, novels, poems, memoirs, plays, letters, children's books, and other similar artifacts. That is, they might be so-called professional writers. But they might also have other profiles. For instance, in awarding the Nobel Prize to Dylan, the Stockholm Committee celebrated his talent as a folk singer, that is, a musician and balladist. Equally, standup comedians such as Jackie Mason and Jerry Seinfeld are storytellers whose diatribes are infused with Jewish humor. Graphic novelists like Art Spiegelman explore topics like the Holocaust in visual form, just like filmmakers such as Woody Allen deliver cinematic narratives bathed in Jewish pathos. Translation and the work of literary critics also fall inside the purview of Jewish literature. It could be said that such amorphous interpretation of literature undermines the entire transition; if the written word is what writers are about, evaluating everything else under the same criteria diminishes its value. Yet it must be recognized that, more than half a millennium after Gutenberg, our definition of the word *book* as an object made of printed pages is obsolete. In the early twenty-first century, books appear in multiple forms.

I now turn to the second question: What makes a Jewish book Jewish? The answer depends on three elements: content, authorship, and readership. While none of these automatically makes a book Jewish, a combination of them surely does. Take, for example, Shakespeare's play *The Merchant of Venice* (1605). Shylock, its protagonist, might be said to be a sheer stereotype of a money lender, even though, in truth, he is an extraordinarily complex character who, in my view, ought to be seen as the playwright's alter ego. Clearly, the play does not belong to the shelf of Jewish literature per se, despite its ingredients. Now think of Kafka's *The Metamorphosis* (1915), in which the protagonist, a middle-class man called Gregor Samsa, wakes up one morning, after uneasy dreams, to discover himself transformed into a giant insect. Nowhere in the novella does the word *Jew* appear. Yet it is arguable, without struggle, that a Jewish sensibility permeates Samsa's entire odyssey, from his feeling of psychological ostracism, within his family and in the larger society, to the perception that he inhabits a deformed, even monstrous body.

To unlock the Jewish content of a book, the reader, first, must be willing to do so. But readers are never neutral; they have a background and an agenda. It is surely possible to ignore Kafka's Jewish sensibility, yet the moment one acknowledges it, his oeuvre magically opens up an array of unforeseen interpretations connecting it to Jewish tradition. Paul Celan, the German poet of "Todesfuge," in an interview in the house of Yehuda Amichai, once said that "themes alone do not suffice to define what's Jewish. Jewishness is, so to speak, a spiritual concern as well." Hence, one approach might be what Austrian American novelist Walter Abish is looking for when asking *"Wie Deutsch ist es*?": How German is this Prague-based writer? Another approach is to move in the reverse direction, questioning how Jewish it is, without an address. Simple and straightforward, the plot line might be summarized in a couple of lines: the path of Jews as they embrace modernity, seen from their multifarious literature, is full of twists and turns, marked by episodes of intense euphoria and unspeakable grief; at times that path becomes a dead end, while at others it finds a resourcefulness capable of reinventing just about everything.

To the two questions just asked, a third needs to be added: What makes modern Jewish literature modern? The entrance of Jews into modernity signified a break with religion. According to some, this started to happen in 1517, when Martin Luther posted his *Ninety-Five Theses* and initiated the Protestant Revolution, which eliminated priests as the necessary intermediaries to God. Or perhaps it happened when, in the Renaissance, at roughly 1650—the date is a marker more than anything else—Europe as a civilization broke away from the long-held view that the ecclesiastical hierarchy justified everything. In my view, the date ought to be 1492. That is when Christopher Columbus sailed across the Atlantic Ocean and the same year Jews were expelled from Spain. Large numbers of them and their descendants, persecuted as they were by the Spanish Inquisition, sought refuge in other lands, including the Americas, fostering a new age of discovery and free enterprise.

In any case, by 1789 the ideas of the French Revolution—*liberté, egalité, fraternité*—were seen as an invitation to all members of civil society, including Jews, to join ideals of tolerance in which an emerging bourgeoisie, the driving force against feudalism, promoted capitalism. New technologies brought innovation, including the movable letter type pioneered by Johannes Gutenberg, which made knowledge easier to disseminate. The outcome was a process of civic emancipation and the slow entrance of Jews to secular European culture—indeed, Jews were granted full civil rights within a few years of the French Revolution. A well-known example of this journey, from the strictly defined religious milieu to the main stage of national culture, is Moses Mendelssohn, the eighteenth-century German philosopher, who, along with his numerous descendants, underwent a series of important transformations quantifiable as concrete wins and losses. A Haskalah champion, Mendelssohn, in his book *Jerusalem* (1783), argued for tolerance and against state interference in the affairs of its citizens, thus opening a debate in Europe about the parameters of tolerance. He translated the Bible into German: his version was called *Bi'ur* (Commentary) (1783).

Mendelssohn's invitation for Jews to abandon a restricted life and become full-fledged members of European culture was a decisive event. It triumphantly opened the gates, so to speak, to an age of mutually respectful dialogue between a nation's vast majority and its vulnerable minorities, the Jews among them. A couple of generations later, one of Mendelssohn's grandchildren, German composer Felix Mendelssohn, known for an array of masterpieces like the opera *Die Hochzeit des Camacho* (1827), was at first raised outside the confines of the Jewish religion but eventually baptized as a Christian at the age of seven. Such a transgenerational odyssey is emblematic of other European Jews: from devout belief to a secular, emancipated existence, from belonging to a small minority to active civil life as a minority within a majority. It is therefore crucial not to conflate modernity with Enlightenment: whereas the former is a historical development that fostered the quest for new markets through imperial endeavors that established, depending on the source, a satellite of colonies, the latter was the ideology behind it.

A forerunner of this crop of scholars is Hayim Yosef Yerushalmi, whose short book, *Zakhor: Jewish History and Jewish Memory* (1982), I thoroughly admire. One of the conclusions drawn from his central arguments is that Jews remember not in chronological ways, but through myth. That is, memory is not lineal; it leaps back and forth with little cohesiveness. The art of telling history depends on sequential narratives: A leads to B, which in turn becomes C. Myth takes the opposite route: it is nonsequential and has little interest in cause and effect. Jewish literature is a way for Jewish memory to engage with history. Emerging from a specific time and place, writers—poets, playwrights, novelists, memoirists—are in dialogue, overtly or unconsciously, not only with their precursors but also, magically, with their successors. Not arbitrarily, Jews are called *Am Ha-Sefer,* Hebrew for "People of the Book." The term was first applied to them in the *Qur'an*—in Arabic, *Ahl al-Kitāb.* Taken together, the books Jews have written in modernity constitute an uber-volume that features them as authors, characters, and reader and that conveys the experience of aterritoriality (even counting those books produced in Israel) as a transcendent endeavor.

Chapter 1
After the expulsion

Until the end of the fifteenth century, Jews outside of the Middle East lived dispersed all over Europe. The various governments offered special dispensation for them to settle in specific areas. In Spain, those areas were called *juderías*, most of which were neighborhoods in larger urban areas such as Toledo, Gerona, and Córdoba. A large community developed in the Iberian Peninsula. Over time, the contact between the three Abrahamic religions— the other two are Christianity and Islam—gave place to what came to be known as *La Convivencia*, which, according to scholarly debates, goes from the Muslim Umayyad conquest of Hispania in the early eighth century until the expulsion.

Prior to 1492, the foundation behind this outlook was a cadre of experimental poets writing in Hebrew that favored a type of liturgical poem called *piyut*, meant for use in religious services. They include Shmuel Hanagid, who, aside from writing poetry, was a military figure, a Talmudic scholar, and a merchant of immense importance in Muslim Spain, and Shlomo ibn Gabirol, known in Latin as Avicebron. He was primarily known for his poetry, portions of which have been integrated into the Yom Kippur liturgy. Yet in European intellectual circles, his work *Fons Vitae*, written in Arabic (its title is *Yanbu' al-Hayat*), was well known, although his authorship was acknowledged only in the mid-nineteenth century. Moses ibn Ezra, who wrote substantially about rhetoric, especially the use of metaphor, differed with Maimonides and was arguably the most important philosopher and biblical commentator of Jewish Spain.

Perhaps the most resonant of the Jewish poets in medieval Spain was Yehuda Halevi, a physician, poet, and philosopher whose book *Kitab al-Ḥujjah wal-Dalil fi Nuṣr al-Din al-Dhalil* (completed in 1140), known in its Hebrew translation by Judah ibn Tibbon as *Sefer ha-Kuzari*, is built as a dialogue between a rabbi and the king of the Khazars. It is an essential philosophical disquisition on various aspects of Judaism, such as the names of the divine, how the universe was created ex nihilo, the value of the oral tradition, and so on. Along with Maimonides's *Guide for the Perplexed* (ca. 1190), Halevi's treatise is of fundamental importance in medieval Jewish theology. Likewise, his diverse poetic explorations are influential. He wrote love poems, elegies, riddles, travel verses, and laudatory poems about friendship, a number of which have been canonized in Jewish liturgy as Shabbat hymns. One of the most enchanting and a primer of the Sephardic outlook is "My Heart Is in the East." It displays, in full splendor, the forking paths of Sephardic identity:

> My heart is in the east, and I am in the far-away west.
> How can I savor food? How might it be sweet to me?
> How might I render my vows and bonds, while
> Zion is under the might of Edom and I am in Arab bondage?
> It would be good for me to leave behind all goods from Spain
> while I behold in my eyes the precious dust of the forsaken sanctuary.

Halevi represents diaspora life for Jews as a forking path between their individual location, in his case, Spain, and Jerusalem, the site of King Solomon's destroyed temple, as the source for constant longing. In the context of aterritoriality, that dualism is a constant. Toward the end of his own life, having lived in various locations in Christian and Muslim Spain, he traveled to Egypt and from there set off for Jerusalem. He probably made it, although

8

rumors have it that he died at sea. It is also said that he was killed by an Arab horseman.

Although premodern when judged by the parameters of the European Enlightenment, these cadres of Hebrew poets continue to exert enormous appeal among Jewish readers. Heinrich Heine, the German Romantic poet and among the first Jews to enter a national literary canon (even though, as in the case of Mendelssohn's descendants, Heine's family converted to Lutheranism when he was young), was infatuated with them to such an extent that he translated some of them into German. Emma Lazarus used Heine's versions as her source for her English versions.

The road to Spain as a unified nation exacerbated the tension among the three religions. The year 1492 is an annus mirabilis when everything fell apart. It marks the time in which *La Reconquista*, the drive to homogenize Spain under a Catholic faith, brought together King Ferdinand of Aragon and Queen Isabella of Castile, known as *los reyes católicos*, the Catholic monarchs, meaning their partnership was based on an agreement established by the Catholic Church. Harassment against Jews and Muslims intensified. Other European nations had already expelled them from their midst: England in 1290, the Duchy of Austria in 1421, and Ravenna in 1491. Others would quickly follow suit: Portugal in 1496, Nuremberg in 1499, and several papal states in 1569. In other words, there was a continental rush to narrow the path minorities—especially Jews—had in emerging nationalistic projects.

The defining characteristic in pre-1492 Spain was the perfidious role that *El Santo Oficio*, the Spanish Inquisition, played in every aspect of life. As an institution, it pushed non-Catholics to either convert or leave. Those choosing conversion sometimes embraced it wholeheartedly. Others engaged in it only as a public act, keeping a hidden identity in the domestic realm, thus living a

9

double life. As the question of *limpieza de sangre*, purity of blood, became a referendum in Spain on people's identity, a new class of people, known as *conversos*, meaning converts, spread all over the Spanish kingdom. The nomenclature includes important variations on the *converso* type: *cristiano nuevo*, New Christian; *marrano*, describing a *converso* in a derogatory sense; its Hebrew equivalent, *anusi*; and Crypto-Jew, a hidden Jew. Aside from the Alhambra Decree, as the Edict of Expulsion is known, other important events took place that year. In an effort to find a new maritime route to India, which was impeded by a Turkish blockade in the Mediterranean Sea, the Genoese admiral, whose ancestry has been suggested to have been partially Jewish, sailed from the Canary Islands to the Caribbean. With funds from Queen Isabella, Columbus set foot on the island eventually known as Hispaniola, now divided between Haiti and the Dominican Republic.

The end of *La Convivencia* dispersed Jews to a number of places: from the Netherlands to Italy, from the Balkans to Turkey and Northern Africa, or Jerusalem and its surroundings, and into the Western Hemisphere. Ladino, also known as *Judezmo* and *judeo-español*, was a language made of Spanish and Hebrew elements and until the late nineteenth century was written in Hebrew characters, though there was a flourishing Ladino publishing industry (using Hebrew characters) well into the twentieth century. Ladino was used to create poetry, lyrics, and storytelling. An emergent consciousness came to the fore, which might be called "the *converso* split," a dense web of transnational connections among *cristianos nuevos*, who possessed Jewish family roots but had abandoned them, yet felt united by the ostracism they were subjected to. They were rejected not only by the Spanish Inquisition and the old Christian majority of Spanish society, but also by Jews. Metaphorically, this group suddenly became the new Jews, a loosely defined people with strong cultural ties, who took it upon themselves to help each other, at times quietly and at other times overtly, against adversity.

Through conversion, those whose genealogy included Jewish elements often became devoted Catholics. This switch was projected into their work. They embedded secret messages in their work to alert readers about the double consciousness they inhabited. Poets like Santa Teresa de Jesús and Fray Luis de León, the latter the author of important exegetical works on the *Book of Psalms* and other biblical narratives, were to various degrees suspected of Judaizing. The same ought to be said of the anonymous author of *Lazarillo of Tormes* (1554), a novel considered the first in Europe in the picaresque genre. The acerbic critique it makes of the Catholic Church was possible only through some distancing from it, which is what *conversos* experienced in their daily life. The same goes for Fernando de Rojas, author of *La Celestina* (1499). The entire narrative is made of a series of dialogues that follow the tradition of courtly love. One of its protagonists is a hybrid between a healer and a matchmaker. If one takes a narrow view of Sephardic culture, all these authors should not be considered part of it. After all, they or their ancestors had abandoned the Jewish faith. Yet that duality, to be an outcast while retaining a certain sensibility connected to one's past, was a feature—religious, intellectual, and emotional—a number of them manifested.

The case of Baruch Spinoza, the Dutch philosopher responsible for the *Tractatus Theologico-Politicus* (1670), is pertinent. He himself rejected his Judaism; as punishment for his ideas, the Amsterdam community in which he lived proclaimed a *herem*, an excommunication. Nobody was allowed to relate to him. Still, his Jewishness defined his worldview. And that worldview, especially in the realms of ethics and government, was the cornerstone in the shaping of essential documents like the US Constitution, written during the Philadelphia Convention in 1787. Américo Castro, a prominent early twentieth-century Spanish cultural historian, author of *The Structure of Spanish History* (1954), concluded that the New Christian mentality was shaped by a sense of pride, not shame, in secrecy. He even speculated, without any tangible evidence, I should add, that Miguel de Cervantes Saavedra, author of *Don Quixote of La Mancha* (1605–15), might have had Jewish blood. A few scholars read the first sentence of his novel—"En un lugar de la Mancha de cuyo nombre no quiero acordarme, no ha mucho tiempo que vivía un hidalgo de los de lanza en astillero"; in my English translation: "In a place of La Mancha of which name I do not care to remember, there lived, not long ago, a hidalgo who has a lance on the shelf"—as evidence of attempting to hide one's origins.

One of the most significant Sephardic writers, whose odyssey showcases the tortured nature of a double life forced by the Spanish Inquisition, is Luis de Carvajal the Younger. He arguably is the most famous martyr of the Spanish Inquisition in the Americas, which, although not as lethal as its counterpart in the Iberian Peninsula, nevertheless established a similar reign of terror. Carvajal's uncle, the Spanish-born, Crypto-Jewish governor of the northern Mexican state of Nuevo León, was aware that in New Spain, as Mexico was known in the sixteenth century, the Spanish Inquisition was more lenient. The uncle brought along his extended family, asking them to retain their secret Jewishness at home. Among them was Luis de Carvajal the Younger, who became known under his chosen name, Joseph Lumbroso, a.k.a. *El Iluminado.* He rediscovered his Jewish roots in his early twenties and became obsessed with them. Never having read the Hebrew Bible, he taught himself a few tenets he discovered in it. Soon, he became convinced he was a biblical prophet endowed with the task of bringing back to their old faith those members of the tribe who had distanced themselves from it.

As Carvajal began to proselytize among other Crypto-Jews in New Spain, the Spanish Inquisition tracked his activities. He, his mother, and his sister were eventually arrested and put in prison. They were interrogated by inquisitors who wanted to know every detail of their endeavor. To extract precise information, they were tortured. Inside the prison, Carvajal communicated surreptitiously

1. Luis de Carvajal the Younger was arguably the most prominent Crypto-Jew to be burned at the stake by the Spanish Inquisition in Mexico. Shortly before his death in 1596, he wrote a memoir that is the first-known autobiographical narrative by a *converso* in the New World.

with his relatives by sending them messages in mamey peels. The inquisitors intercepted these messages. The Carvajals repented, at least publicly. The story takes a surprising twist. Carvajal was released from prison, at which point he proselytized again. And he drafted an autobiographical narrative in which he described in detail—in the third person—all his activities, including his and a friend's decision to circumcise themselves on the bank of the Panuco River. That narrative is the first memoir by a Jew written in the New World. Not long after, Carvajal and his relatives were arrested again and burned at the stake, in the Plaza del Quemadero in downtown Mexico City, in the most important auto-da-fé ever to take place in the Americas. (Against the background of a lost manuscript, the graphic novel illustrated by Steve Sheinkin, *El Iluminado* [2012], recounts his ordeal.)

As Sephardim built new communities, their literature reflected the historical events affecting them. One example is Daniel Levi de Barrios, a.k.a. Miguel Barrios. Born in Spain and wanting to connect with his Jewish heritage yet understanding he needed to keep it secret, he escaped the Inquisition by traveling to Algeria, Italy, France, and then the West Indies. Levi de Barrios serves as a connection with the nascent Ottoman Empire under Suleiman the Magnificent. It was there that the movement known as *Sabbatanism*, in which Levi de Barrios participated, took shape. Its central figure was Shabbetai Zvi, the false messiah, a rabbi, and kabbalist from Smyrna, in the Ottoman Empire, whose claim to be the messiah persuaded thousands of followers. In the year 1666, just as his prophesy of a new age was to arrive, he was arrested in Constantinople by the grand vizier Ahmed Köprülü. While in prison, Zvi converted to Islam. His unexpected move shocked his followers. Some abandoned Judaism; others followed him in conversion, creating a subwing of the movement that, in its antinomianism, argued for sin as a road to salvation. (In 1967, Gershom Scholem wrote a lucid biography of Zvi and his movement.) The impact on Levi de Barrios was deep. As a convert, he looked at Zvi as a redeemer like Jesus Christ. But after the conversion to Islam, he became an antinomian, becoming persuaded that redemption was attainable through sin. He set out to write a treatise—now lost—on the divine presence in the modern world. Afterward, he kept his distance from all types of religion. In time, he became a successful poet as well as the author of *comedias* and history books. Whereas Carvajal was himself convinced of, and ultimately doomed by, his messianic powers, Levi de Barrios, getting his feet wet on Shabbetanism, emerged from the experience as an astute champion of enlightened ideas. This duality would define successive generations: some would fear doom while others would embrace hope.

In the eighteenth and nineteenth centuries, Sephardic writers included Benjamin Disraeli, who was baptized at an early age and displayed little interest in Judaism, and, on the opposite side, Grace Aguilar, a novelist, poet, and advocate for religious and education reform whose most important poems meditate on the biblical characters of Hagar and Ishmael. But unlike Yiddish literature, which I discuss in the following chapter, the Sephardim never fully developed a coherent modern literary tradition. Instead, there are figures here and there who acknowledge the Spanish heritage as impacting their oeuvre.

Among them is Greek-born Swiss novelist Albert Cohen, who worked for the International Labor Organization and wrote humorous, idiosyncratic novels, like *Belle du Seignior* (1988), full of idiosyncratic Ottoman characters. These two positions, rejection and embrace, are notable across the tradition. Arguably the most famous twentieth-century Sephardic writer is Bulgarian novelist and cultural critic Elias Canetti, who grew up in Ladino but wrote in German. Quite prolific, he alternated between novels and book-long essays. His most famous novel is *Die Blendung* (1935), known in English translation as *Auto-da-Fé*, a phantasmagoric exploration of life under fascism. His two most important nonfiction books are *Masse und Macht* (1960), known as *Crowds and Power*, a probing study of the psychology of the masses under fascism; and *Der andere Prozess* (1969), titled *Kafka's Other Process* (1969) in English, in which he explored, in minute fashion, the sentimental life of the author of *The Metamorphosis* with his lover Felice Bauer. Canetti's style could oscillate from the lyrical to the phantasmagoric. This is clear in his multivolume autobiography, especially in *Die Gerettete Zunge* (1977), translated as *The Tongue Set Free*. The reader is able to sense a delicious mix of Ladino, German, and English, and the respective cultures they represent, in its pages.

Other Sephardic writers include Italian activist and member of Parliament Natalia Ginzburg; chemist and Holocaust survivor Primo Levi, also Italian; and Serbian short-story writer Danilo Kiš, who spent the last period of his life in France. Born in Palermo, Sicily, a prominent anti-fascist and for a while a member of Italy's Communist Party, Ginzburg's work focuses on the tension between the domestic and public spheres in Italian family life, especially among the intelligentsia during the Second World War. Her novel *Family Lexicon* (1963) is a vivid, surgically delivered, empathetic portrait, with an added focus on family language, that is anchored in the death of Leone Ginzburg, an influential anti-fascist journalist, editor, writer, and teacher and Natalia Ginzburg's first husband. It chronicles the plight of Italian Jews under the regime of Benito Mussolini and the death of celebrated poet Cesare Pavese, whom she published while an editor in Turin at the publishing house Eunaudi. Ginzburg (née Natalia Levi) also published Primo Levi, Italo Calvino, and another Sephardic writer, Carlo Levi, author of *Christ Stopped at Eboli* (1945).

Influenced by Bruno Schulz, Jorge Luis Borges, and Vladimir Nabokov, his volumes of stories *A Tomb for Boris Davidovich* (1976), about betrayal and deception in the Soviet bloc, and *The Encyclopedia of the Dead* (1983), a postmodern meditation on tyranny, are lucid instances of this tradition. A. B. Yehoshua, the Israeli novelist, sought to understand the continuity between the expulsion in 1492 and a sprawling Sephardic family tree in his epic novel *Mr. Mani* (1989). Faulknerian in language as well as in structure, it tells the story of various generations in reverse chronological order, with the youngest descendant, an Israeli, starting the tale, and the last one, an Iberian, concluding it.

It is important to make a distinction between this tradition and its Mizrahi counterpart. The latter term describes Jews from Middle Eastern and North African descent. After the destruction of the Second Temple, as Jews were exiled in the Roman Empire, a very small number stayed in Jerusalem and the surrounding areas and persisted in their religious practices. The expulsion from Spain also brought Jews into North Africa and the Middle East, which means that a portion of Mizrahim have Sephardic blood. Occasionally in their work, Iraqi-born Israeli author Sami Michael and Tel Aviv-based Orly Castel-Bloom delve into the junction between the forking paths of Sepharad and Magreb.

An ethereal quality present in Mizrahi literature is personified—if such a verb might be used to describe such a ghost-like individual—in Monsieur Chouchani. While I confess to knowing almost nothing about him, not even his first name, let alone his date of birth, I feel the urge to include him in this survey. He was a rabbi, a Talmudist, and a conversationalist who deliberately left no trace, especially in published form. Two major Jewish thinkers of the twentieth century, Emmanuel Levinas and Elie Wiesel, about whom I will reflect in depth later, befriended him in Paris. Wiesel, upon finding out Monsieur Chouchani had died in 1968, procured a proper Jewish tomb and burial in Montevideo, Uruguay, where he passed away. He apparently had a prodigious mind and was able to recite entire sections of the Talmud. Yet he lived, by all accounts, an itinerant life and was often homeless. In countless ways, his existence is symbolic of the wandering ways of Mizrahi, and for that matter all, Jewish literature.

The most wide ranging of Sephardic authors is Angelina Muniz-Huberman. A refugee of the Spanish Civil War, her family moved to France and subsequently to Mexico, where she went to school. Her household was Catholic. One day, Muniz-Huberman saw her mother sweep the kitchen. She took the garbage she piled in the center not through the door, but through the window. When the daughter asked why, the mother responded that it was a custom she had learned as a girl. Eventually, Muniz-Huberman figured out such behavior was frequent among Crypto-Jews. This led her to a voyage of discovery. She eventually became a scholar of Jewish mysticism, a poet, and a novelist whose oeuvre, such as *The Confidantes* (1997), deals with the legacy of secrecy among *conversos*. In her work, she returns to the medieval Hebrew poets—Hanagid, ibn Gabril, ibn Ezra, and Halevi—to find continuity. She empathizes with Iberian writers such as Santa Teresa de Jesús and Fray Luis de León, and she connects with kabbalists and other mystics.

Abraham Joshua Heschel, the Polish-born American philosopher and civil rights activist who wrote a biography of Maimonides (1935), once published an essay suggesting that the Sephardic sensibility is precise, almost mathematical, and allergic to expressions of disquiet and nervousness and that it sees itself best reflected in liturgical chants. While these might be generalizations, Sephardic literature indeed oscillates toward certain motifs and moods. One is the motif of the lost key. It symbolizes an abandoned door that belongs to the past, although nobody remembers exactly where that door is located. The key invokes nostalgic moods and shares a feeling that the family is both the conduit for continuity to last and its saboteur. Along the way, the key showcases an urge for travel by a people with shifting diasporic addresses to find connections across borders to be able to replicate certain patterns of religious behavior.

Chapter 2
The Yiddish self

As the Sephardic diaspora was taking root, another Jewish center was already in development: *Ashkenaz*. It is a reference to Germany, Austria-Hungary, France, and the Pale of Settlement, the region in Poland, Lithuania, Latvia, Ukraine, Belarus, and Russia in which the Russian czar allowed Jews to settle under particular restrictions. Yiddish (also called *yidish taich*, the Jewish German, and *der mame loshen*, the mother's tongue) was initially a mix of German and Hebrew written in Hebrew characters. It became a portal in which their Ashkenazi angst was crystalized, the language of the eastern European collective self as it seized its place in the world. Although there is much debate about the origins of Yiddish, it was likely born around the ninth century. What is unquestionable is that in the context of Jewish languages, with the exception of Hebrew, it is by far the most developed and has a standardized syntax. Within a few centuries, Yiddish became the lingua franca of about twelve million people. There were a number of varieties in different regions: Litvak, Galitzianer, Warshaver, and so on. By the twentieth century, a number of sociolinguists, lexicographers, and other scholars of language developed projects to appreciate all these nuances. The father-and-son duo of Max Weinreich, who wrote a two-volume history of the Yiddish language, and Uriel Weinreich, who published a popular modern Yiddish/English English/Yiddish dictionary, are among the most significant.

Yiddish was already around when Dante's *The Divine Comedy* was being written. Among the earliest works in Yiddish literature are a translation, via the Italian, of a chivalry romance, *Buoyo d'Antona*, by Elijah Levita. There are knight-inspired stories about Kings David and Solomon and the *Mayse-bukh* ("Storybook," 1602), a compendium of stories, sayings, and rabbinical tales. More significant is the biblical commentary targeting women, called *Tzene Urene* (1616), written by Jacob ben Isaac Ashkenazi, still popular in the early twenty-first century. In its early stages, Yiddish was perceived as the language of women, children, and an illiterate Jewish population. As such, it was looked down on by Talmudists and the rabbinical elite. The supporters of the Jewish Enlightenment called Haskalah were the *Maskilim* (meaning enlightened). They were active in a variety of fields, among them education, philosophy, economics, politics, and religion. Many of them made their case for assimilation in European languages. On the other end were the *Hasidim* (in Hebrew, the word *hasidut* means piety), most of whom were poor, rural inhabitants devoutly committed to a religious life. Yiddish was their medium.

At its core, Hasidism was a reaction to the stiff Talmudic tradition that focused on rigid intellectual debate among sages, highlighting semiotic interpretation and mnemonic powers. As communal leaders, some rabbis, from the Hasidic perspective, had become aloof, disengaged, and interested in remote topics. At the same time, a mystical countercurrent was exemplified by significant books such as the *Sefer ha-Zohar* (thirteenth century), written by Moisés de León, and by figures like kabbalists such as Isaac Luria. They preached *avodah be-gashmiyut*, worship through corporeality. Nurtured by these mostly secretive teachings, Hasidism sought to bring to the masses an ecstatic religious experience through stories, chants, and other forms of communal engagement. But the folksy image of the movement is deceitful. It was embraced by authorities in the religious and financial world, from populist rabbis to entrepreneurs. A flank among the Maskilim, called the *Misnagdim*, looked at Hasidism, in its rejection of modernity, as a step backward. Through schools and pamphlets, they attacked Hasidism as an awkward, dangerous, ill-conceived movement that, in the end, would only serve to delay, if not altogether undermine, the advancement of Jews in European society.

A couple of distinct characteristics made Hasidism a singular movement. The first is the role of storytelling as a complement, at times even proxy, for the communication between the divine and human realms. Storytelling acquired a performative quality that infused the individual in the act of praying with theatrical characteristics. Instead of looking at storytelling as an aspect of religion that is intimate and domestic, done in a private setting, it became part of the texture that brought communities together. Except for those stories attributed to particular *rebbes*, such as Israel ben Eliezer, a.k.a. Ba'al Shem Tov, an itinerant rabbi said to have performed magic, Hasidic tales are anonymous. There were thousands of folk tales, delivered orally in Yiddish, and these were eventually written by down by some kind of disciple or amanuensis. The transition resembles the ancient journey of oral stories, like the Torah itself, and in other civilizations like the poems of Gilgamesh, *The Odyssey*, and *The Mahabharata*. Yiddish did not have a high-brow, aesthetic quality; instead, it delivered its message in practical, straightforward terms. The relationship between master and pupils and apprentices took center stage.

Much of what we known about the Ba'al Shem Tov is based in myth emerging from the oral tradition. Historians argue, contrary to popular belief, that Hasidism was far from a movement exclusive to the indigent class. After an initial period of reticence, powerful authorities embraced it. The second characteristic is the transformation of the rabbi's role from a Talmudic erudite into a healer and storyteller endowed with quasi-supernatural powers. This position was based on the belief that the divine presence manifests itself in nature and that one might be able to commune with that presence through mystical encounters. Over the centuries, compendia have been published of Hasidic stories, including retellings by Elie Wiesel. One of the most significant compendiums was by German philosopher Martin Buber, whose oeuvre has a decisively existential quality. In his forties, he collected almost one hundred stores in a two-volume anthology called *Tales of the Hasidim* (1933). The first volume is dedicated to what Buber called the early masters, active until the early nineteenth century, and the second to the late masters, who lived from the 1880s onward. Interested in the relationship between God and man, or, as he puts it in one of his most famous titles, *Ich und Du* (1923)—in English, *I and Thou*—Buber saw Hasidic storytelling as spiritual dialogue.

As the Hasidic tradition evolved, several single Hasidic masters became authors themselves, or almost. The most sophisticated, in content as well as style, is Rabbi Nachman of Breslov, a great-grandchild of the Ba'al Shem Tov. *Sipurey Ma'asiyot* (1816), a volume known in English simply as *Tales of Rabbi Nakhman*, contains twelve of his stories, which he delivered orally and were transcribed by his scribe Nathan Sternhartz, a.k.a. Nathan of Nemirov. These tales are built as allegories about the destruction of religious life brought about by modernity. An example and one structured as a folk tale is "The Rabbi's Son" (1816). It describes the journey, overt as well as intimate, of an existentially dissatisfied young man who comes to the conclusion that his only path for enlightenment is through a meeting with a rabbinical sage who lives in a distant town. The young man asks his father for permission to visit the sage, but his father dissuades him from embarking on the journey. The young man does try several times to reach the rabbinical authority. On the way, a series of mishaps takes place that prevent him from achieving his objective, including a meeting with a mysterious character at a tavern where the young man eats while on his way. The conclusion of the story is that, had the young man, described as a "small light," met the sage, a "large light," the entire world would have been redeemed. Rabbi Nachman's stories are built on paradoxical structures. For starters, several of them rotate around kings, queens, princes, and princesses, characters that belong to fairy tales and have little connection to post-biblical Jewish life. They feature archetypes like the devil (*yetzer ha-rah* or "evil inclination"), who appears to people to destabilize their existence. A truthful life is a test of conviction as well as the result of a series of accidents. His secular admirers included Franz Kafka.

Concurrent with Hasidism as a popular movement were other early literary manifestations in Yiddish. Among the most enduring is the memoir of Glikl. She was born in Hamburg in the middle of the seventeenth century and lived through a period of dramatic transformation, from plagues to economic upheaval. A magnificently resourceful Jewish woman, Glikl reinvented her place in Europe. Glikl, sometimes described as Glikl of Hamel, wrote her five-book memoir not for posterity but for a very concrete audience: her family. The enduring power of the narrative has much to do with her astounding talents as a writer. This is an invaluable historical document about domestic life between 1691 and 1719. With a strong sense of self conveyed in interwoven anecdotes, Glikl writes as a way to confront her life as a widow. The gravitational center in the family, she beholds tradition and displays financial acumen as she confronts countless challenges from her environment.

A dramatic shift in Yiddish culture—call it maturity—took place in the mid-nineteenth century. Several writers, dreaming themselves equal to major novelists in France, England, Spain, and Italy, sought to develop a distinct Jewish literary tradition, one that made Jews feel like a nation as well. Jewish theater began to take shape. The Yiddish golden age revolved around three hugely important figures. The first in that group was Sholem Yankev Abramovitch, a.k.a. Mendele Mokher Sforim, Yiddish for Mendele the book peddler (in Yiddish literature, pseudonyms abound); Itzkhok Leib Peretz; and Shalom Naumovich Rabinovich, a.k.a. Sholem Aleichem.

Mendele, whose oeuvre, when compared to those of Sholem Aleichem and Peretz, has been eclipsed by the passing of time, spent his youth as the helper—what Sephardic Jews call *lazarillo*—for an itinerant beggar who wandered through Belarus, Ukraine, and Lithuania. His experience shaped his views of how Jewish life in *shtetls*, a small Jewish village across the Pale, was undermined by corrupt rabbinical figures. His early work, like the play *Di Takse* (1869), in English *The Tax*, was denunciatory in tone. Mendele saw literature as a tool to educate the masses. But as his career evolved, he took a more esthetically sophisticated viewpoint, using language as a humorous resource to highlight the contradictions of Jewish life. His innovative novels, including a satirical tribute to *Don Quixote*, called *Travels of Benjamin the Third* (1878), meditate on diasporic Jewish life.

Peretz is the second component of the nineteenth-century Yiddish literary triptych. An anti-universalist, he did not believe Jews were unique, that is, the chosen people. Instead, writing plays, poems, essays, and stories in both Yiddish and Hebrew, he argued for an approach that emphasized distinctness. He believed in the power of folklore and, unlike many Maskilim, admired the authenticity he found in the teachings of the Hasidic masters. Among his most famous works are the poem *Monish* (1888) and the allegorical play *At Night in the Old Marketplace* (1907). A prime example of Peretz's approach to modernity is his story "If Not Higher. . . ." The plot explores the tension between rationalism and spirituality. The protagonist is a Jew who, rumor has it, disappears on Saturdays without a trace. One night, a Litvak (i.e., a Lithuanian Jew, who were known for their skepticism) follows the protagonist. He sees how early in the morning the Jew changes his Sabbath clothes, enters the forest in the form of a *muzik*, and brings wood to an old lady who is ill in bed. After performing his good deed, he returns to town once again in mysterious, unencumbered ways, puts his Sabbath clothes on, and goes on with his life. A humble, silent act of kindness has been performed without regard to flashiness.

שלום-עליכם.

2. Sholem Aleichem's novel *Tevye the Dairyman*, a collection of related stories—the first one appeared in 1894—is about the plight of a poor *shtetl* dweller as he sees each of his daughters marry a suitor. It is the centerpiece of modern Jewish literature.

Unquestionably, the most important Yiddish writer from the period and perhaps of all time is Sholem Aleichem. Sometimes described as the Jewish Mark Twain (or should it be the other way around, Twain being the American Sholem Aleichem?), his versatile style, full of humor and compassion, succeeded in humanizing perfectly discernable social types: the devout if inquisitive *shtetl* dweller, the small-city *luftmench*, the rascal rabbi's son, the talkative train traveler, and so on. With time, Sholem Aleichem's cast of characters has become ingrained in the collective Jewish imagination, so much so that it is a lens through which late nineteenth-century Yiddish civilization is accessed.

Having considered rabbinical ordination, Sholem Aleichem opted for a career as a writer with a penchant for humor. A prolific author—he wrote novels, stories for children and adults, essays, and more—his legacy almost single-handedly is based on one book, *Tevye the Dairyman* (starting in 1894). Made of a series of interconnected stories set in the fictional *shtetl* of Anatevka (they were published in a single volume in 1912), it is the most famous Yiddish novel ever. Tevye, the protagonist, is a paragon of the average poor country dweller. He has several daughters. Since the installments were published haphazardly without much consideration to narrative coherence, in some parts he is said to have five daughters and in others up to eight.

Throughout the narrative, Sholem Aleichem depicts the interaction between the Anatevka Jews and the Russian *muzhiks*. Anatevka, more so than its counterpart Yehupetz, a surrogate for Kiev, the Ukrainian capital, which Sholem Aleichem also fictionalized, comes across as a forerunner of William Faulkner's Yoknapatawpha County and Gabriel García Márquez's Macondo, the mythical town on Colombia's Caribbean coast. Yet it is at the level of language where Sholem Aleichem's novel actually thrives. The scaffold is a multilayered dialogue in which Tevye himself delivers the story, in supreme detail, to Sholem Aleichem himself. In other words, the installments of the novel are presented as instances of first-person narrative targeting a specific recipient. Tevye constantly meanders, imbuing each plot with constant references to Torah, the Mishna, and Talmudic misquotations. But he is a poor peasant with a limited education. His numerous references result in countless misquotations. This strategy allows Sholem Aleichem to showcase the connection between religion and folklore among Yiddish speakers. The Jewish masses might not have received a proper education, yet they were tuned to a wide range of textual references. Tevye, the reader feels, is a kind of improvised rabbi, enormously humane in his approach to life even if only partially cognizant of his sources. The immediate reception of *Tevye the Dairyman* was enthusiastic.

Mendele, Peretz, and Sholem Aleichem brought Yiddish literature wide recognition. In intricate ways, they emphasized its connection with ancient sources while pushing it to embrace the standards of other European national traditions. Among the most important Yiddish writers at the turn of the twentieth century was ethnographer, political activist, playwright, and cultural commentator Shloyme Zanvl Rappoport, a.k.a. S. Ansky. Born in Chashnicki, in today's Belarus, he was a Socialist who wrote in Russian and Yiddish. He is best known for two works among many: The first is the multivolume *Khurbn Galitzie* (published posthumously in 1922), a travelogue through Galicia during the First World War, a treasured document of a community about to be drastically transformed by history. Ansky and his ethnographic team record interviews and other snapshots with poor Yiddish speakers in countless *shtetls*. He turned the material into a multilayered narrative known in English as *The Enemy at His Pleasure*. The second, Ansky's dominant work, is his play *The Dybbuk, or between Two Worlds*, first performed in 1920. Most of it is about an exorcism to liberate a woman from the demon that inhabits her. A Yiddish-language movie adaptation of *The Dybbuk* was made in 1937, directed by Michał Waszyński, who also made films in Poland, Italy, Spain, and the United States. In the style of German expressionism, it is considered one of the most significant films in the history of Yiddish cinema.

As Jews left eastern Europe between 1880 and 1930, a fertile Yiddish literature emerged in places such as New York City, where it was connected with the plight of the masses, from poverty to enlightenment. Writers published their stories in newspapers and other periodicals, and readers became avid followers. In Russia, it thrived even after the Bolshevik Revolution, when there was a drive to align the ideological message under the rubric of socialist realism. Yet Joseph Stalin, whose anti-Semitism was no secret, waged a war against Russian Jews. He declared Birobidzhan, near Siberia and on the Chinese border, a Jewish autonomous region and ordered Yiddish, along with Russian, to be the region's official language. Clearly, it was all a ploy to ghettoize the Jewish population. Tragically, Stalin even went after numerous writers. On the night of August 12–13, 1952, known as the Night of the Murdered Poets, thirteen of the most prominent Jewish writers and scientists in the Union of Soviet Socialist Republics, including

Dovid Bergelson and Peretz Markish, were executed. Another crucial voice, Pinchus Kahanovich, a.k.a. Der Nister, was sent to the Siberian gulag. In New York, *Forverts*, the Yiddish name for the Socialist newspaper *The Jewish Daily Forward*, was among the most important literary outlets.

Among the writers who continued writing in Yiddish out of loyalty toward *di mame loshn* or because their immigration took place rather late, or both, is Polish-born Jacob Glatshteyn. He arrived in New York City before the age of twenty and rebelled against the structured diet of Jewish themes in Yiddish literature, seeking more flexible, at times exotic, topics. And Lithuanian Chaim Grade, part of the aesthetic group called "Yunge Vilna," Young Vilna, produced gorgeously styled narratives that paid tribute to his Orthodox education. After the Second World War, he stayed in Europe until he immigrated to the United States in 1948. Glatshteyn and Grade did not produce a distinctively immigrant literature. Israel Joshua Singer, the older brother of Isaac Bashevis Singer, also did not specifically write about immigration, at least not to the degree that his brother did.

On staff at the *Forverts*, I. J. Singer was a writer of an enormous narrative breadth similar to Fyodor Dostoyevsky's. Singer's novels offer panoramic historical views of families across generations. Set in Łódź, Poland, *The Brothers Ashkenazi* (1936) tells the story of a pair of siblings from a Hasidic background whose personalities are dramatically different: one is outgoing and entrepreneurial; the other is introspective, even mystical. Their paths are seen against the backdrop of the end of the First World War, the Bolshevik Revolution, and other major events. Likewise, *The Family Carnovsky* (1943) is the study of the various members of a Jewish family in Germany as Adolf Hitler is ascending to power. As time goes by, these novels retain their vitality, in part because of I. J. Singer's dexterous literary style.

Before the second half of the nineteenth century, there was little by way of Jewish theater. The closest Yiddish speakers came to witnessing drama on stage was the Purim *shpiel*, a reenactment, meant for children, of the biblical *Book of Esther*. Russian-born Avrum Goldfaden in a span of four decades wrote more than three dozen plays. By the time Yiddish immigrants were settled in New York in the thirties, Yiddish theater, with actors like Boris Tomashevsky, who started in adaptations of Harriet Beecher Stowe's *Uncle Tom's Cabin* and Shakespeare's *Hamlet* (called *Der Yidisher Bokher*, the Jewish student), was one of the most lucrative artistic forms, touring to other American cities like Chicago and Los Angeles and even abroad to places like Warsaw and Buenos Aires.

The most popular Yiddish writer in America for a while, one who did write about immigration yet never switched to English, was Sholem Asch. There is no doubt that he was the most popular Jewish writer in America for some time—*Der Man fun Natsres* (*The Nazarene*, 1939) appeared in English before it did in Yiddish and was a Book-of-the-Month Club main selection. He outsold all other Yiddish writers in the United States in translation until Isaac Bashevis Singer won the Nobel Prize in 1978. His sprawling, bestselling novels like *East River* (1946) told the story of immigrants to New York. Asch's interest in Jesus Christ and other characters of the New Testament, which crystallized in novels like *The Nazarene*, *The Apostle* (1943), and *Mary* (1949), offended scores of Yiddish-language readers, especially since these works were published just as the Second World War was unfolding on the European stage. Among Asch's most controversial work is the play *God of Vengeance* (1922). It was the first time two women kissed, not only in a Yiddish play but also on Broadway, where the play premiered in 1923. The English-language American Jewish playwright Paula Vogel wrote a play, *Indecent* (2015), offering a female perspective on how Asch's play came to be. When compared to Yiddish literature in the Pale, its equivalent in America was populated by a generous number of accomplished women writers, among them Celia Dropkin, Rokhl Korn, and Kadya Molodovsky.

Even though Yiddish might be said to have almost died in the Nazi gas chambers, another fate almost as devastating swept it in America: assimilation. Within a couple of decades, as the children of immigrants went to public schools, where they adopted English as their primary language, its survival was in question. By the sixties, *Forverts*, with a circulation at its height of around two hundred thousand copies, became a shadow of its old self. Other cultural outlets also lost gravitas. In the twenty-first century, Yiddish, among secular Jews, is a source of nostalgia. There are drives to study the language in order to revive its vitally. Yet it is a daily tongue almost exclusively used among ultra-Orthodox Jews in Williamsburg and Crown Heights, New York, but also in Jerusalem, including in the neighborhood of Bnei Brak, thousands of whom see themselves as direct descendants of various Hasidic sects.

Chapter 3
The age of anxiety

The invitation to embrace Jews as full members of modernity
generated much anxiety, internally as well as in society at large.
That anxiety filtered into literature in the form of nightmarish
narratives. It did not happen overnight. Instead, it came about as
a result of dramatic changes at the end of the nineteenth century.
Scientific explorations of how the mind worked, and of psychiatric
methods of addressing mental illness, brought along fresh
understanding of the human mind. At the forefront was a Jewish
doctor in Vienna named Sigmund Freud, who would become the
father of a new school of thought known as psychoanalysis. Early
on, Freud was interested in hysteria. His experiments with
patients led him to believe dreams were not garbled images, but
nuanced manifestations of the unconscious with symbolic
meaning.

In *The Interpretation of Dreams* (1899), he offered a number of
case studies that served as the foundation of a method developed
by Freud whereby patients explored the tension between
conscious and unconscious life. A number of his patients were
Jewish. Writing as a scientist with a clear, commanding style that
addressed not only his peers but also a general audience, his
investigations opened up unexplored horizons in the realm of
psychology. They also posed broad ethical questions about how
masses behaved. Although he was ambivalent toward Judaism,

Freud's Jewish identity was dear to his heart. Throughout his life, he wrote about a number of biblical themes. In his book *Moses and Monotheism* (1939), he proposed that the theological innovations of the Israelite political leader Moses, who orchestrated a slave revolt against the pharaoh, were less original in their religious conception than most people thought. Freud argued that Moses, in his monotheism, was only a surrogate of Akenathen, another pharaoh, this one from around 1350 BCE, who first proposed replacing a constellation of multiple deities with a sole omnipotent, invisible one. An avid reader, he also delved into literature, like Greek drama and Shakespeare's plays, to explain behavioral patterns. His career developed as the rise of anti-Semitism, a fixture of Jewish life in Europe, increased notably at the end of the nineteenth century. By the end, Freud needed to flee to London with his family to escape the expanding forces of Nazism.

Interest in how time is understood, in physics as well as in philosophy, brought about new theories. Henri Bergson, a Jewish French philosopher, argued that time is always experienced subjectively. Albert Einstein, the German-born Jewish theoretical physicist, brought down the conception that time is linear with his general theory of relativity. Einstein had a pantheistic view of the universe as divine similar to Spinoza's. He believed "in a God who plays dice" and "in complete law and order in a world which objectively exists" and which he, "in a wildly speculative way," was trying to comprehend. Plus, the analysis of how money moves around, how it is accumulated in a few hands, and its connection with how nations take shape and how they are ruled was the topic of another Jewish thinker, one who rejected outright his heritage. Marx's economic study *Das Kapital* (1867), at the center of which was a broad-stroke theory of history, helped unleash revolutionary forces that precipitated historical change. Particularly in Germany, England, and the Russian Empire, Nationalists, Socialists, Communists, anarchists, nihilists, Marxists, and others fought for power. Although Marx's father had converted to Protestantism before Karl was born, he still falls within the realm of Jewish thinkers.

As is often the case, Jews were at the center of these debates not only as theoreticians but also as targets of animosity in a mass culture obsessed with conspiratorial anti-Semitism. Spurious pamphlets like the anonymous *The Protocols of the Elders of Zion* (1919) claimed Jews like Marx, Freud, Einstein, and others were intent on controlling the world's finances. Arguing along similar lines, in the United States Henry Ford's four-volume pamphlet *The International Jew*, distributed in the twenties, sought to orchestrate a global campaign. All this anxiety—the human heart is made of dark chambers, time is relative, and money corrupts—materialized in the work of secular Jewish writers, including Marcel Proust, whose multivolume novel *À la recherche du temps perdu* (1913–27), known in English translation as either *Remembrances of Things Past* or *In Search of Lost Time*, is a monumental exploration of memory and time. The father of Proust (full name Valentin Louis Georges Eugène Marcel Proust) was a prominent epidemiologist, and his mother was the daughter of a rich Jewish family from Alsace. His worldview was shaped by the Dreyfus Affair, an anti-Semitic scandal in France between 1894 and 1906 in which an army captain, Alfred Dreyfus, was wrongly accused, and subsequently convicted, of treason. The events around the affair ratified for Proust the precarious place of Jews in French culture. The leading character of Charles Swans in his novel, a doomed Jewish stockbroker who becomes an art critic and dealer, is often understood to be Proust's double.

Anxiety is at the heart of the work of three European Jewish writers, one Czech, one Russian, and one Polish: Franz Kafka, Isaac Babel, and Bruno Schulz. None wrote in a Jewish language; instead, they excelled in the language of their respective cultural milieu. And they all died tragic deaths. Their work offers an increasingly sobering sensation of doom. Kafka is the high rabbi of modernity. His oeuvre is by turns pessimistic, even cynical, and

33

mystical, designed to foster transcendence. He might be read as a prophet of despair and the proclaimer of the end of religion as well as a champion of endurance, enlightenment, and resolve at a time of impending danger. While he worked for an insurance company, he dreamed of literature. But he felt he was banished from its halls. His entire career, one might say, was spent in the shadows, obsessed with physical transmutations and bureaucratic labyrinths. A citizen of Prague, he did not even write in its language; he wrote in high German, the language of the Czech educated elite.

An endless river of ink has been spilled by way of interpreting Kafka's work. His followers, tacitly and obliquely, include Borges, Nabokov, Isaac Bashevis Singer, J. M. Coetzee, and Haruki Murakami. His novel *The Trial* (1925) appeared under the aegis of the small avant-garde Belin publishing house Verlag Die Schmeide. Subsequent books were released by the Munich publisher Kurt Wolff. They sold poorly. These works were made available in the years preceding the Nazi ascent to power. Then, between 1933 and 1938, laws made it impossible for Jewish authors to be published in Germany. But the Jewish publisher Schocken Verlag, sponsored by a department store magnate, somehow avoided the ban as long as its books were meant only for Jewish readers. Reluctantly at first, Schocken brought out Kafka's writing, ultimately making a commitment to bring out his entire oeuvre. As the Second World War broke out, Schocken needed to relocate in Palestine; from there it moved to New York, where it opened an office in 1945. It was only after the war that Kafka came to be considered a major twentieth-century literary voice, his books becoming classics. Hannah Arendt, the German exile who moved to New York in 1941, worked as an editor for Schocken and was instrumental in making Kafka available in English, understanding his place in posterity. "Though during his lifetime he could not make a decent living," Arendt wrote in a letter dated August 9, 1946, "he will now keep generations of intellectuals both gratefully employed and well-fed."

It has been said that Kafka is less dazzling than Marcel Proust and less innovative than James Joyce, but more painful and perhaps more universal than either. In the canon of modern Jewish literature, his novella *The Metamorphosis*, about middle-class nervousness and about the Jewish body being perceived as monstrous, might be said to be its center of gravity. Through he is never described as Jewish, the protagonist, Gregor Samsa, in his vulnerability and marginalization, represents the diaspora. He is physically different—that is, "animalistic," meaning not fully civilized—an alien as well as a member of a minority. He is in tension with his own family, maybe even his ancestry. Samsa exists within a dream he cannot understand. And he thinks that if he sleeps longer, he could perhaps forget all the nonsense he experiences.

Another piece by Kafka also referring to transmutation is "Report to an Academy" (1917), in which Red Peter, an ape who has learned how to behave like a human, describes, in front of a scientific audience, how he achieved the makeover. It was originally published in *Der Jude*, a Zionist magazine edited by Martin Buber. Especially given this fact, the story has been read as a critique of diasporic Jewish life and a satire of Jewish assimilation to European civilization. Yet one more celebrated work by Kafka is *The Process* (1912). It is about Joseph K., who, as the narrative begins, is arrested. The key to the plot is that Joseph K. is guilty but he does not know why. The plot is about his trials and tribulations through the bureaucratic ordeal. And there is *The Castle* (1926), about a character, known only as K., who attempts to travel to the seat of government in his city but never achieves his objective. Also significant is the unfinished novel *Amerika* (1927). It originally started as a short story called "The Stoker" that centers on the adventures of a sixteen-year-old European immigrant called Karl Roßmann, in a land like America, except that Kafka never visited the United States. He also wrote a number of parables. The one I identify with the most is "Before the Law," in German *"Vor dem Gesetz."* Part of *The*

3. In *Die Verwandlung* (*The Metamorphosis*, 1915), by Franz Kafka, the protagonist, Gregor Samsa, undergoes a mutation that might be a metaphor of Jewish diaspora existence.

Process, it tells the story, in barely a page, of a man who waits outside a gate to be allowed in. A guard stands next to the gate deciding who is and is not allowed in. The man's intention is to enter through the gate, but he is stopped repeatedly. Years go by. Toward the end he discovers the gate was made for him never to traverse it.

The imagery is frightening: Kafka's message is that we are excluded from paradise, even though we ourselves created the idea of paradise. In an aphorism, he states, "The crows assert that a single crow could destroy the heavens. This is certainly true, but it proves nothing against the heavens, because heaven means precisely: the impossibility of crows." It seems ironic that through his oeuvre—most of which, by the way, the author asked his close friend novelist Max Brod, before his death, for a last request: that everything he left behind in the way of manuscripts, diaries, sketches, letters, and so on be burned unread (boxes with Kafka's archives ended up in Israel in the hands of a descendant of Brod's secretary, closed to the public for years because of litigation)— Kafka never actually uses the words *Jew, Jewish*, or anything similar. However, these terms are ubiquitous in his journals, correspondence, interviews, and other nonfiction. He meditates on Jewish alienation, the sense of living in the cultural margins, overwhelmed by higher social, political, and religious forces. Kafka also explores spiritual topics that in significant ways connect his themes to those of Hasidic storytelling as exemplified, among others, by Rabbi Nachman of Breslov. In any case, such is Kafka's influence, that the adjective "Kafkaesque" is used frequently. It is taken to mean alienation, especially in connection with a nightmarish bureaucratic process. Merriam-Webster defines the words as "having a nightmarishly complex, bizarre, or illogical quality." Only the names of very few writers become adjectives. Kafka died of tuberculosis, at the age of forty-one, in a sanatorium in Kierling, Klosterneuburg, Austria. His death passed unnoticed by literati until decades later. Since then, he has been a staple of school curricula worldwide.

The second prophet of anxiety is Isaac Babel. Born and raised in Odessa, on the Black Sea, he left behind a small oeuvre made predominantly of short stories in the line of Maupassant. His two most important titles are *Red Cavalry* (1926) and *Odessa Stories* (also 1926). In different ways, they explore the life of Jews under the Soviet regime, which Babel endorsed, even though, under Josef Stalin, he became a victim of it. He was forced into silence after a speech he delivered in 1934 at a congress of the Soviet Writers' Union and died in one of the dictator's purges against

Jewish intellectuals. At the age of forty-six, he was executed at Moscow's Butyrka prison. *Red Cavalry* explores Babel's experience in Semyon Budyonny's 1st Cavalry Army during the Polish–Russian War in 1920. During this time, he kept a diary. He also used the material as inspiration for his collection of stories. Babel's most significant passages are about his role as a Jew. He meditates on the perception that Jews are incapable of physical work, that they are given to intellectual endeavors and are seen as weak. In a milieu where stamina is essential, the challenge offers an unequaled understanding of diaspora life. In contrast, *Odessa Stories* is a collection of tales about mob boss Benya Krik, who ruled over one of the city's Jewish gangsters. The stories are set in the Jewish ghetto of Moldavanka. Benya Krik is at once a daring and outstanding literary creation. This is not the first time a Jewish writer, addressing a non-Jewish audience, features a villain, however sympathetic that character might be. Babel is not afraid to expose Krik's odious side. In doing so, he gives him credence and actually humanizes him.

One of Babel's most daring, accomplished stories in the latter volume is "Story of My Dovecot." It centers on the plight of a young Jewish boy with top high school grades who is nevertheless deprived from a place because of *numerus clausus*, a method whereby universities limited the number of a particular group of students. He is told by his father that "he must remember everything." The plot unfolds on the day the boy goes to the market to get a dove given to him by his parents in reward for his academic excellence. The notorious pogrom of October 20, 1905, unravels around him. He witnesses the social fabric of his own town collapse. As chaos and violence strike, the boy must find his way home while protecting the dove near his chest. Babel's style is precise, almost mathematical. He does not indulge in overwrought emotions. The action is described from the viewpoint of an innocent child who cannot quite make sense of the ruinous world that surrounds him or explain why he and his family are being especially targeted.

The third and last Jewish minister of misfortune is Bruno Schulz, who aside from writing also liked to draw. Cumulatively, his oeuvre feels like a phantasmagoria taken from a Brueghel painting. Schulz uses in his brief yet richly designed scenes—he only left behind two books, *The Street of Crocodiles* (1934), also known as *Cinnamon Shops*, and *Under the Sign of the Hourglass* (1937), along with a number of essays, stories, and dispersed notes as well as a substantial number of drawings and even a mural—to present an imaginative picture of life under German occupation. The first book was composed in postcards Schulz sent his friends Władysław Riff and Debora Vogel. The scenes pertain to a Jewish family that owns a textile shop. There are sections about a marketplace and about an imposing father and the decadence of the Austro-Hungarian Empire. Nothing much happens. There are mystical elements and intricate dream sequences. Schulz's verbal style is intense. Like Kafka, Schulz has a special place in Jewish literature. His odyssey has been the topic of a handful of novels, including *See Under: Love* (1986), by Israeli writer David Grossman, about a child who imagines himself connected to Schulz. And Cynthia Ozick's *The Messiah of Stockholm* (1987) is about the manuscript Schulz was purportedly working on when he was killed. In Ozick's novel, the novel suddenly shows up in Sweden's capital, which is the place where the Nobel Prize for Literature is presented. Just as in the cases of Kafka and Babel, Schulz's life story is, in itself, what makes his ordeal essential in Jewish literature. He was at an impossible crossroads during the Second World War: being Jewish and being Polish. It is clear from his oeuvre that his genius emerged from the negotiation between these two identities. He was shot in 1942, at the age of fifty, in his hometown, Drohobycz, then in Poland and now in Ukraine, by a Nazi.

It was the middle of the Second World War. Kafka had died twenty years earlier and Babel barely two years before. Unease about Jews was pervasive. They had become targets, symbolizing the collapse of the European dream of tolerance. The Holocaust was under way.

Chapter 4
Shoah and memory

The systematic destruction of six million Jews and the culture they had built for centuries in Europe—known in Hebrew as the *Shoah*—took place within a short span of time. Its reverberations are infinite. The scope was so large, it defied conception. In the decades after 1945, a torrent of memoirs were published about the harrowing experiences. Holocaust museums were built, in Jerusalem; Washington, DC; Berlin; and elsewhere, to sum up the knowledge of what happened. Memorials multiplied. Video libraries featuring interviews with survivors were compiled. In other words, almost from the beginning, and even as the massacres were taking place, efforts had begun to accumulate testimonials. Theodor W. Adorno, a philosopher and musicologist, whose Jewish father had converted to Protestantism, wrote that after Auschwitz it was barbaric to write poetry. And as facts about death camps were revealed, a slew of deniers began to orchestrate a campaign to insist the calamity never happened.

Unlike most other modern Jewish literature, the one emerging from the Holocaust asks to be taken on its own terms. It is not designed to be aesthetically pleasing. In fact, dispensing judgment about its quality seems wrong. What matters is that it exists as a statement against oblivion. Arguably the most famous chronicle, not of crematoria per se but of a life in hiding, is Anne Frank's *Diary of a Young Girl* (1947). Among the earliest narratives of

Nazi persecution, it tells the story of a precocious thirteen-year-old in Amsterdam living in a secret annex (*Achterhuis* in Dutch) with her family and four other people, chronicling her isolation in the rear of the seventeenth-century canal house, as German soldiers roam the streets. Frank was a writer with a clear, precocious style. Her journal depicts her vulnerabilities in tender, caring ways. The fact that she, her mother, and others in the attic ultimately died in Auschwitz and other death camps adds pathos to her tale. Her father, Otto Frank, rescued the diary and, after the war, saw it through publication, but not without controversy. As novelist Meyer Levin wrote in his nonfiction book *The Obsession* (1974) and others also argued, Frank might have loved his daughter and wanted her voice to be heard. But the strategies he embraced to achieve his goal were not without blemish.

As it happens, he expurgated from Anne's prose direct references to her Jewish upbringing. What he was after, apparently, was universalizing the diary at the expense of Jewish particularism. In doing so, he deprived her of the very reason she and others like her had been targeted: her cultural background. The Broadway adaptation, as well as the Hollywood film that followed it, was equally biased. In these productions, Frank was a universal hero of resistance. She herself might have been shaken by such an act of censorship. Not until 1995 did an unabridged edition of the diary appear. Her Jewishness was restored. Anne Frank became an emblem of innocence, purity, and sanctity. The Amsterdam house where she hid became a tourist attraction. What if she had survived? Philip Roth, who called her "Kafka's lost little daughter," imagined this possibility in his novel *The Ghost Writer* (1979). Scores of other writers, musicians, and filmmakers have also used art to reflect not only on her tribulations but also on how memory itself shifts over time.

A similar fate surrounded another prime example of Holocaust literature, *Night* (1956), by Elie Wiesel. Part of a trilogy that includes the lesser known titles *Dawn* (1961) and *Day* (also 1961), this brief autobiographical novel might be seen as the next installment of Frank's journals. Along with his family, Wiesel was sent from his hometown, Sighet, in Romania, to Auschwitz in 1944. He might have crossed paths with the Dutch girl. Wiesel's mother and younger sister died there, while his two older sisters survived, as he did.

Immediately after the war, having written the manuscript of *Night* in Yiddish (a student of Kabbalah, Hasidism, and the Talmud, he knew Yiddish and Hebrew, aside from Romanian), he published it in Argentina as the *Poylishe Yidntum* series. It was while he lived in Paris as a journalist and after he had it translated into French that he sent the manuscript to Andre Malraux, a novelist, art critic, and France's minister of cultural affairs. Malraux recommended it for publication, but not before damaging references to Germans were taken out. The version readers received, therefore, left out direct criticism of Nazism. Wiesel instead concentrated on his own odyssey. The artistic sacrifice was beneficial: the novel brought him worldwide acclaim, becoming essential reading about the Holocaust. Did the journey of *Night* from its original to its accepted adaptation constitute a betrayal? Was this another attempt at universalization? One might simply describe it as the usual cleanup a book undergoes before it reaches the printer. Yet behind the cutting one might also find a desire by Wiesel to shed unnecessarily polemical layers to make himself more palatable to a larger pubic. It is all a sign of the times, for as he matured in the limelight, his voice as a witness of the Holocaust became part of the collective consciousness of the twentieth century. He did not stop criticizing the victimizers, though he made sure he did not target the postwar Germans, the children of the Nazis, who were eager to close the door on a horrific chapter of their nation's history.

Fittingly, Primo Levi's *If This Is a Man* (1947), known also as *Survival in Auschwitz*, is a haunting narrative written by a precise, scientific mind, though it is neither cold nor unemotional.

(Levi's book *The Periodic Table* [1975] is a scientist's memoir that uses the periodic table of the elements as a springboard to reflect on a Jewish young man's dreams of becoming a chemist before the Second World War.) Of Sephardic ancestry, Levi was a chemist in Turin, Italy, when the Nazis deported him. His chronicle is laconic and humble. The Holocaust novellas of Aharon Appelfeld, for example, *Badenheim 1939* (1978), almost always told from a child's viewpoint, are spare and hallucinatory. Even more frugal—maybe the term is *septic*—is *Fatelessness* (1975), by Hungarian author Imre Kertész. There is a basic difference, especially when it comes to the Holocaust, between autobiography like Anne Frank's diary and fiction like Wiesel's *Night*: one is anchored in reality, and the other leaps from it as it lets the imagination do the job. They are equally truthful.

This is not the case of a countergenre that purported to be truthful yet was based on lies, which fed the thirst of Holocaust deniers. There are two infamous cases. One is *The Painted Bird* (1965), purportedly based on horrifying episodes in the itinerant life of its author, Polish-born Józef Lewinkopf, a.k.a. Jerzy Kosiński, an esteemed American writer who, among other prestigious positions, was president of the American chapter of P.E.N. A thorough journalistic investigation found Kosiński's life story to be bogus. The second is *Fragments: Memoirs of a Wartime Childhood* (1995), written in German by Swiss clarinetist Bruno Dössekker, under the pseudonym of Binjamin Wilkomirski, who was found to have concocted his Holocaust recollections in therapeutic sessions. It is important to state that although Kosiński's narrative was a concoction (it has been suggested that someone other than Kosiński wrote it), he was indeed hidden as a Jew in Poland during the Second World War and survived the atrocities. In contrast, Wilkomirski merely believed he was a survivor.

Other Holocaust texts come with less baggage. Belarus-born Yiddish writer Avrum Sutzkever, called by some the greatest poet of the Holocaust, was sent to the Vilna ghetto. Just before it was liquidated, he joined the *partisaners* who fought against the Nazis. Sutzkever survived and testified at the Nuremberg Trials after the conflict. He proved Adorno wrong by producing, in *Burnt Pearls* (1981), poetry that reads like a howl. His poignant poem "Under Your White Stars," a meditation on divine intercession, is one of the most popular Yiddish songs that came out of the Holocaust; it was written in the ghetto and set to music by Abraham Brudno as part of the play *Di yogn in fas*, in English *The Hunt in the Barrel*, a parody of Diogenes. In its plea for renewal, it is reminiscent of the work of Berlin-born Nelly Sachs, who, unlike Wiesel, grew up in an affluent Jewish household. A romantic at heart, the Nazi ascent to power left her speechless, incapacitating her from talking, pushing her to mental illness. Sachs escaped to Sweden with the help of her friend, writer Selma Lagerlöf. Her Holocaust poems offer a vision of spiritual transcendence. Sachs shared the Nobel Prize with Sh. Y. Agnon.

The most emblematic poem emerging from the Holocaust is by Romanian-born, German-speaking Paul Celan, a major postwar poet—and friend of Nelly Sachs—who believed the Holocaust had driven Europe to the abyss. In thirty-six lines, "*Todesfuge*," known in English as "Death Fugue," ruminates on the role musicians played in camps as death took its toll. The poem was published in a Bucharest literary magazine in 1947. It depicts a commander who orders concentration-camp prisoners to work while a musical orchestra plays on. The two female characters are the commander's beloved Margarete and Shulamit, whose name invokes the biblical *Song of Songs* and who represent the image of ideal beauty from the Aryan and Semitic perspective The oxymoronic motif of black milk permeates the poem. The plural "we" meditates on Germany as a nation indulging in barbarism. Is there any hope left? In times of despair, Celan pointed to language as the only palliative. "Only one thing remained reachable, close and secure amid all losses: language," he said; "Yes, language. In spite of everything, it remained secure against loss. But it had to go through its own lack of answers, through terrifying silence, through the thousand darknesses of murderous speech. It went through. It gave me no words for what was happening, but went through it. Went through and could resurface, 'enriched' by it all." Unsurprisingly, Celan's poetry became more cryptic as time went by. His last works, including *Atemwende* (1967), are almost impenetrable, in large part because as a Holocaust survivor he found life undecipherable, which ultimately led him to commit suicide.

Fundamental to Holocaust literature are crime investigations. None is more polemical than Hannah Arendt's *Eichmann in Jerusalem: A Report on the Banality of Evil* (1963), which was furiously debated when it was first published in book form. Arendt was a German refugee in New York who had once been a student and lover of Martin Heidegger, a prominent German philosopher with Nazi sympathies. She had made her career studying totalitarianism. When Adolf Eichmann, one of the world's most prominent Nazis, was spotted in Buenos Aires, he was kidnapped and flown to Tel Aviv in a secret operation orchestrated by the Israeli espionage agency, the Mossad. Israel's first prime minister, David ben Gurion, ordered the operation. An international uproar followed, but Israel put Eichmann on trial.

In her work, Arendt was interested in the role individuals play in totalitarian states, how they are hypnotized by the leader, how they embrace consent, and how they lose the capacity to discern between truths and lies: in short, how they went from individuals to masses. She explored the function of propaganda, the embrace of evil as a conduit for a false version of good. And she was interested in what came to be known, in the Trump years, as "fake news": the use of media to create ideological silos in which followers are fed predictable news by a leader. Arendt wanted to understand obedience, passivity, and compliance, that is, how freedom gives way to submission. She argued, in reaction to

4. Hannah Arendt in New York City, to which she immigrated in 1941. A lucid thinker about totalitarianism, democracy, and freedom, Arendt was commissioned by the *New Yorker* to report on the trial of Nazi criminal Adolf Eichmann in Jerusalem.

Emmanuel Kant's book *Religion within the Bounds of Bare Reason* (1793), that "Niemand hat das Recht zu gehorchen"—no one has the right to obey.

She got herself assigned to write a report on the trial for the *New Yorker* magazine. The result was a chronicle that, in the eyes of some, blamed Jews as victims, downgraded Eichmann to a mere government apparatchik, and, equally significant, pondered aloud whether Israel, as a young nation born from the atrocities committed during the Second World War, ought to endorse capital punishment. Should those who were victims take revenge at a time when the world was seeking a return to normalcy? Countless rebuttals to *Eichmann in Jerusalem* were published as op-eds and letters, on radio and television shows, and in books. The controversy felt as if there was an international campaign to discredit Arendt on the grounds that her loyalty as a Jew to her people was questionable.

The most important articulator of such an approach was Gershom Scholem, an old acquaintance of Arendt and at that point a professor of Jewish mysticism at Jerusalem's Hebrew University. He accused Arendt, in a letter dated June 1963, of lacking "*ahavath Israel*," a love for the Jewish people. "There is something in the Jewish language that is completely indefinable, yet fully concrete—what the Jews call '*ahavath Israel*,' or love for the Jewish people. With you, my dear Hannah . . . there is no trace of it." He added, "I regret that, given my sincere and friendly feelings toward you, I have nothing positive to say about your theses in this work." Arendt responded in the following months. Her answer was a detailed, point-by-point rejoinder: "How right you are that I have no such love," she stated, "and for two reasons: first, I have never in my life 'loved' some nation or collective. . . . The fact is that I love only my friends and am quite incapable of any other sort of love. Second, this kind of love for the Jews would seem suspect to me, since I am Jewish myself. I do not love myself or anything I know that belongs to the substance of my being."

How the Holocaust is translated into other media is also significant for Jewish literature. Perhaps one of the most popular examples is the innovative graphic novel *Maus* (1991), by Art Spiegelman. Although the launching point is Spiegelman's troubled present-day relationship with his father, a survivor, it reached into the past by portraying Nazis as cats and Jews as mice. Its publication, first in serialized form and then as a book, had a profound effect, especially on young audiences. It felt liberating in that it allowed popular culture—the graphic novel is seen as a pop artifact—to tackle as serious a theme as the Holocaust.

After the Signal Corps footage showing images of piled-up corpses in newsreels preceding movies throughout the United States immediately after the war, documentaries like Alain Resnais's *Night and Fog* (1955) emerged, one of the first to delve deeper into these images. Along with Claude Lanzmann's exhaustive 566-minute *Shoah* (1985), it is an example of visual narratives to make a case about forensic evidence. Steven Spielberg's *Schindler's List* (1994) and Roman Polanski's *The Pianist* (2002) adapted important books to the screen, reaching larger audiences who, by the turn of the twenty-first century, only had a fragile knowledge of the atrocities.

A troubling question had emerged by then: Might the second generation and those not directly linked to the Holocaust have the right to continue telling the story? This became the issue when Cynthia Ozick's *The Shawl* (1980), made of the eponymous story published in the *New Yorker* on May 26, 1980, as well as a longer narrative called "Rosa," was released. Ozick was not personally affected by the Holocaust. Most of her information came from books, movies, and other sources. Inspired by a reference in William L. Shirer's *The Rise and Fall of the Third Reich* (1960), *The Shawl* is about the relationship between a mother, her baby daughter, and her niece in a death camp. Out of food and in despair, the mother feeds the hungry baby with a shawl, which is the only item she has available. As readers questioned Ozick's authenticity, claiming that her portrait of the inhumanity Jews lived through felt stilted, she, a polemicist, finally decided, to the degree possible, to distance herself from the story. The battles for who gets to shape memory had defeated her.

A significant twenty-first-century addition to Holocaust literature is the novella *The Memory Monster* (2017), by Israeli lawyer and novelist Yishai Sarid. It actively addresses the passing of memory about the Nazi atrocities to a next generation in Israel, at a time in which the Jewish nation manifestly distances itself from its origins, including the Holocaust trauma. The son of a prominent journalist and politician, Sarid builds the plot in a way that is reminiscent of Kafka's story "A Report to an Academy" (1917). A young historian offers a report to the chairman of Jerusalem's Yad Vashem museum about his experience leading youngsters to the extermination camps. These trips are common in Israel as an effort to deliver an actual experience instead of simply offering information about the past in flat, unengaged fashion. The historian's assessment is harsh: young Israelis are not really interested. They take the trip to escape, yielding an adventure with little engagement. Their indifference is apparent as they mindlessly joke about what they encounter.

Chapter 5
Into the mainstream

Emma Lazarus's "The New Colossus," a poem inscribed on a plaque on the pedestal of the Statue of Liberty, welcomed immigrants sailing into New York harbor between 1903 and 1954. The famous last six lines read,

> "Keep, ancient lands, your storied pomp!" cries she
> With silent lips. "Give me your tired, your poor,
> Your huddled masses yearning to breathe free,
> The wretched refuse of your teeming shore.
> Send these, the homeless, tempest-tost to me,
> I lift my lamp beside the golden door!"

These lines are a leitmotif announcing America's relationship with the rest of the world, its stance toward immigration, and its vision of the so-called American Dream, a magnet for a large numbers of poor Yiddish speakers from the Pale in the last third of the nineteenth century. Interestingly, before "The New Colossus," Lazarus wrote another sonnet, titled "1492," that feels strikingly similar in structure and content. The last four lines read,

> "Ho, all who weary, enter here!
> There falls each ancient barrier that the art
> Of race or creed or rank devised, to rear
> Grim bulwarked hatred between heart and heart!"

As Jews, female and male, worked predominantly in sweatshops, living in cramped tenements in the Lower East Side's ghetto, poverty reigned rampant. No wonder the number of activists, like Emma Goldman, who advocated for change—including gender equality and the abolition of marriage—in manifestos and protests.

It was an age of political awareness. A literary record of the immigrant journey, and the conditions in which they lived, soon materialized in the form of stories, poems, novels, speeches, memoirs, and journalistic chronicles. Abraham Cahan, a shrewd socialist opinion-maker, reigned as editor of the *Forverts* for forty-three years. He is best known for the ambitious saga *The Rise of David Levinsky* (1917), written in the realist style of Theodore Dreiser. It tells the story of a Russian Jewish immigrant who renounces his heritage to become an American, only to find himself severed from his roots at the end of his life. Equally important is Anzia Yezierska, the author of the collection of stories *Hungry Hearts* (1920), the novel *Bread Givers* (1925), and the autobiography *Red Ribbon on a White Horse* (1950). Her depiction of the Jewish immigrant's struggle to find a new home, the sense of alienation, and in particular the vulnerability of women in the workplace and as full-fledged citizens is wrenching. Likewise, *The Promised Land* (1912), by educator and immigration activist Mary Antin, showcased her metamorphosis from Russian-born Yiddish speaker to accomplished English-language stylist.

The most accomplished narrative of Jewish immigration is *Call It Sleep* (1934), by Henry Roth. The novel mostly takes place in the Lower East Side. It is told from the viewpoint of David Schearl, a little boy living with his parents in the tenements. He has an intellectual side to him that verges on mysticism. The plot concerns his ordeal navigating his violent father and overprotective mother, his experiences in *cheder* (Jewish religious school), his relationship with various neighbors and acquaintances, and others populating his habitat. Roth began the manuscript in 1930 and completed it four years later. By then Roth, an undergraduate at City University, had met poet Eda Lou Walton, who was an instructor at New York University. He moved into her apartment in Greenwich Village. Her influence was decisive in his quest to become a writer. With a strong social-realist style that embraces a Joycean aesthetic, that is, playfully experimenting with language, the book was published in 1934. It received laudatory notices but was quickly forgotten until it was republished in 1964, championed by Irving Howe. He praised it as an astonishing yet overlooked literary item, a precious account of Depression-era New York that needed to be rescued from the dustbin of history. *Call It Sleep* became an immediate bestseller, selling more than one million copies. It has since been elevated to the status of classic.

After the novel was published, Roth published stories in magazines like *Commentary* and the *New Yorker*, but otherwise disappeared from sight. He was employed at Augusta State Psychiatric Hospital in Maine and was rediscovered in the early 1990s. Rather than stop his literary endeavors, he had continued writing, and in a short span of time, he produced a monumental tetralogy, autobiographical in nature, under the title *Mercy of a Rude Stream* (1994–98). These volumes focus on Ira Stigman, a character much like Roth, and the existential path that takes him from Jewish Irish Harlem onward to a full-fledged American life. At the heart of the novel, and of Roth's disappearance from public view, is a troubling secret: for years, he had been in an incestuous relationship with his sister.

The decisive Yiddish writer in America who serves as a bridge with mainstream, often non-Jewish audiences is Isaac Bashevis Singer. Born Itzjok Singer in a Polish *shtetl* and the younger brother of Israel Joshua—their older sister, Esther Kreitman, was also a memorable novelist, and Moshe, the youngest sibling, died in the Holocaust—he acquired a new immigrant persona,

Bashevis, by adopting his mother's maiden name, Batsheba, as a tribute to her intellectual prowess and rigor. In Poland, he had published in various periodicals and completed a novel about *dybbuks* and other spiritual endeavors, *Satan in Goray* (1935). Finished copies of it did not reach him until he was already in New York. Upon arriving in New York, Singer began a long-standing collaboration with *Forverts*, where he published under a number of pseudonyms. He wrote stories and novels like *The Family Moskat* (1950), which the newspaper serialized and were later released in English translation, in modified, often abbreviated, form. The pivot in Singer's career, and a watershed moment in modern Jewish literature, took place in 1953, when Saul Bellow translated Singer's story "Gimpel the Fool" ("*Gimpel Tam*" in the Yiddish) into English. Suddenly, a fairly mature Yiddish writer (he was almost fifty years old) acquired a considerable following, first made of young, educated Jews who, after the Second World War, were looking for ways to reconnect to the world of their immigrant parents, and later by a broad readership with minimal knowledge of Jewish topics. Singer became for them a kind of *zayda*, a grandfatherly figure.

In her novella "Envy: Or, Yiddish in America" (*Commentary*, 1969), Cynthia Ozick, herself an accomplished American Jewish novelist and critic, created a fictionalized version of Singer to meditate on his impact on the Yiddishist circle in America that included figures like Jacob Glatshteyn, Chaim Grade, and others. What most infuriated them was Singer's penchant for sexual topics. His stories and novels are full of explicit scenes, which in the eyes of his critics were his concession to American taste. As Ozick's character's put it succinctly, he prostituted the entire Yiddish literary tradition. To no surprise, his work appeared not only in magazines like the *New Yorker* and *Esquire*, but also in *Playboy*. In any case, Singer plowed forward. While he continued writing in Yiddish, he forged a unique partnership with an army of translators, a number of whom did not know Yiddish. Prolifically releasing novels and collections of stories, from *The*

Magician of Lublin (1960) to *Shosha* (1978), he became a global celebrity. No Yiddish writer was photographed more frequently. Yet his personal life was built on treacherous secrets. He abandoned his first wife and child in Poland. He married his second wife, Alma, knowing his first might still be alive. He was a liar and a chronic womanizer. And he cheated with people's money.

At any rate, it is a mistake to credit Singer's success to the lurid content he inserted in his oeuvre. The truth is that he was an extraordinary storyteller (although his brother, I. J., was a better novelist). In carefully crafted narratives, he deftly offered audiences a window into the life of Hasidim and Maskilim in the Pale at a time when American Jews were feeling severed from their past. Had he not found a way to communicate with his readership through translation, there is no way to say what that feeling of discomfort would have turned into. The only Yiddish writer ever to be awarded the Nobel Prize, he was an inveterate, versatile storyteller with the capacity to conjure a whole universe in a few strokes.

Acceptance into the American literary canon took place with the second generation, when Jewish American writers moved from traditional immigrant tales to complicated explorations of the unfulfilled promises of the American Dream. The national ethic was work, work, work. The way to achieve it often sacrificed family. Jews were no exception. In *Death of a Salesman* (1949), by Arthur Miller, Willy Loman, an archetype of the broken middle-class man, dreams of a better life for his children yet remains unable to catch up with that dream. The play, a family drama, is the ultimate exploration of the relationship between the individual and society. Although Loman is not explicitly Jewish, nor are any of the characters in Miller's most widely performed play, *The Crucible* (1953), he inaugurated a lineage of probing Jewish playwrights who adroitly explore challenging social issues on stage. That lineage includes Clifford Odets, Paddy Chayefsky, and David Mamet, as well as Wendy Wasserstein, who questioned gender roles in *The Sisters Rosensweig* (1992), and Tony Kushner, whose two-part play, *Angels in America: A Gay Fantasia on National Themes* (1992), fearlessly analyzes the American response to the AIDS epidemic.

Jewish poetry became another genre to inquire about the conflicts America fostered. Aside from Emma Lazarus, with her romantic meditation on American compassion, Karl Shapiro pushed for more openness in ethnic relations, and Adrienne Rich championed changes to the perception of women in society and investigated their Jewishness, sometimes circuitously, in progressive ways. Allen Ginsberg, the leader of the Beat movement since his years as a Columbia student, took an antiestablishment approach that defied conventions. Among his important works is the poem *Kaddish* (1956), in which he pays tribute to his mother, Naomi Ginsberg. Ginsberg often performed in public with musical instruments. Music, indeed, cross-fertilized poetry and vice versa, as is clear in the work of Robert Allen Zimmerman, a.k.a. Bob Dylan. His country ballads, often infused with a strong ideological message, tell stories of love and camaraderie against hardship. In 2016, he was awarded the Nobel Prize for Literature, according to the committee's citation, "for having created new poetic expressions within the great American song tradition." Likewise, the songs of Leonard Cohen, a Montreal-born poet and songwriter, also have a strong ideological message. His convulsive career included periods of obscurity as a result of his drug addiction. Cohen's well-known lyrics in "Hallelujah" are an expression of deeply felt, anti-institutional faith.

Led by diverse figures like Gloria Steinem, Betty Friedan, Tillie Olsen, Grace Paley, and Louise Glück, American Jewish women writers flourished in the second half of the twentieth century, their Judaism mattering to them to various degrees or not at all. Steinem and Friedan did canonical work as feminists. Friedan released the manifesto *The Feminine Mystique* (1963) and

Steinem founded *Ms.* magazine in 1972. Paley had her feisty, conversationalist style. By her own account, she had not set out to be a writer. As a mother and housekeeper in Greenwich Village, one day, finding herself bored, she scribbled down her thoughts; she was also studying literature and writing poetry at the New School with W. H. Auden. A neighbor who was a New York City editor read what she wrote, encouraged her to publish her stories, and eventually helped her collect them in volumes like *Enormous Changes at the Last Minute* (1974). Paley's family spoke Russian and Yiddish, but she grew up speaking English. In Paley's narratives, the reader gets the sense of eavesdropping on someone else's conversation or listening to a person's stream of consciousness. Among the most distilled is "Goodbye and Good Luck," in which an older woman speaks to her much younger niece about her relationship with an older Yiddish actor. First and foremost an activist, Paley was involved in the movements against the Vietnam War and US military intervention in Central America. Her poetry has a distinct ideological approach, finding humanity while pushing a political message.

Cynthia Ozick is on the opposite side of the spectrum. If Paley is a *poet engagé*, Ozick, for whom Henry James's oeuvre was an inspiration, is baroque in style and aloof in her conception of the writer in regard to culture. Her essays from *Art & Ardor* (1986) and *Critics, Monsters, and Fanatics* (2016), and her fiction in novels like *The Puttermesser Papers* (1997), which presents a variation on the theme of the golem from a female perspective, have the cadence of a perfectly mapped hallucination.

Of singular importance is Bernard Malamud. His novel *The Assistant* (1957), its plot drawn from Malamud's childhood in Brooklyn, is about Jewish immigration. And *The Fixer* (1967) deals with anti-Semitism in Russia. In these works, Jewishness is synonymous with American individualism. That is also the lesson from a couple of novelists who represent the apex of mainstream embrace: Saul Bellow and Philip Roth. Bellow was born in

Montreal, Canada, but moved with his family to Chicago as a child. Roth was born in Newark, New Jersey. When they embarked on their careers, they were perceived as ethnic writers; by the time they reached their apex, they were considered national treasures.

Bellow's intellectual odyssey, his fertile engagement with Western ideas, represents the zenith of twentieth-century Jewish literature. In his view, writers have the thermometer that measures culture as it changes, how love and death are understood, how time is conceived individually and socially. Novels were an assemblage of lies that somehow manage to make truth available to readers. Jewish lives, he argued, were defined by accident: "We do not make up history and culture. We simply appear, not by our own choice. We make what we can of our condition with the means available. We must accept the mixture as we find it—the impurity of it, the tragedy of it, the hope of it."

The first line of Bellow's novel *The Adventures of Augie March* (1953) is legendary: "I am an American, Chicago born—Chicago, that somber city—and go at things as I have taught myself, freestyle, and will make the record in my own way: first to knock, first admitted; sometimes an innocent knock, sometimes a not so innocent." Few sentences capture, in such a jazzy way, the zeitgeist of Jews making it in America. Equally memorable is *Herzog* (1964), which revolves around a series of letters the narrator, Moses E. Herzog, writes to an assortment of addressees, including the long-dead Friedrich Nietzsche. The narrative is a tour de force of ideas as they emerge from one emotional wreck after another.

A Nobel Prize recipient, Bellow, a towering Midwesterner with an elastic wit, vigorous engagement with the world of ideas, and passionate embrace of literature vis-à-vis the blindsiding ubiquity of pop culture, was a model Jewish novelist. Personifying the confident, big-city Jew, he embodied the zeitgeist of a book-hungry American obsessed with assessing how ideas were being

5. Along with Bernard Malamud and Philip Roth, Saul Bellow, the author of *The Adventures of Augie March*, brought Jewish literature into the American literary mainstream. His works engaged with influential twentieth-century ideas from the perspective of daily life.

reformulated in the second half of the twentieth century at a precipitous speed. He was dismissive of feminism and critical of multiculturalism. (Toward the end of his life, he purportedly asked, dismissively, who the Tolstoy of the Zulus and the Proust of the Paquans were.) All in all, Bellow's oeuvre might be said to be about the vertigo brought about by Jewish conscience as well as consciousness in modern times.

The mind-bending, multifarious oeuvre of Philip Roth might well be considered the before and after of American Jewish literature. His debut took place in 1959 with the publication of *Goodbye Columbus*. This collection gathered stories exploring a variety of explosive topics about secular Jews in America. For instance, "The Conversion of the Jews" is about a young apostate who, one day during Hebrew school, threatens to commit suicide by throwing himself down if the temple's rabbi does not admit that virgin birth is possible and that they too believe in Jesus's existence. He also forces them to endorse the "turn the other cheek" dogma.

Roth became a household name with *Portnoy's Complaint* (1969), a hilarious meditation of a mother–son relationship seen through the conversations between the son and his therapist. This volume caused a stir among American Jews. Roth wrote books using at least three different alter egos; one was Nathan Zuckerman. The books about Zuckerman include *The Counterlife* (1986), *American Pastoral* (1997), *I Married a Communist* 1998), and *The Human Stain* (2000). The second fictional stand-in for Roth is David Kepesh, featured in *The Breast* (1972), *The Professor of Desire* (1977), and *The Dying Animal* (2001). And a fictionalized version of Philip Roth shows up in *Deception* (1990), *Operation Shylock: A Confession* (1993), and *The Plot against America* (2004). This measured unfolding of a writer's personalities allowed Roth to look at American Jewish life from the perspective of a kaleidoscopic self that is always in motion.

In the context of modern Jewish literature, the last two novels in the list are experiments with fiction that reconfigure historical facts. *Operation Shylock* offers an indispensable link between American Jewish and Israeli literatures. In it, Philip Roth, finding himself in the middle of a severe depression, learns that an alter ego—another Philip Roth—is attracting media attention in Israel. Among other encounters, he meets Aharon Appelfeld, the Holocaust writer. He also learns that the Roth alter ego is promoting the idea of a repatriation of Israeli Jews to Poland, arguing that Israel as a modern state is morally bankrupt. In the novel, a controversial idea is taken to its extreme consequences.

Likewise, *The Plot against America* is set at an alternative time in American history in which Franklin D. Roosevelt is defeated in the presidential election of 1940 by Charles Lindbergh, who unleashes an anti-Semitic atmosphere that impacts the life of the Roth family in New Jersey. The novel was read as an announcement of the Trump years, in which anti-Jewish attacks became rampant in the United States. By the time Roth announced, around 2015, that he was done with literature, the journey of the Jewish writer had reached its climax. Never before had the job of being a writer been as profitable, both financially and in terms of reputation. The journey from the edges to the epicenter of modernity was complete. The proverbial golden door mentioned by Emma Lazarus in "The New Colossus" had unquestionably opened up.

Chapter 6
The Promised Land

The state of Israel represents at once a 180-degree turn in Jewish literature. For starters, it represents an address for the Jewish people; in other words, aterritoriality is summarily rejected. After all, Israel itself is an address, a specific place not only inhabited by Jews, but also run by them. Therefore, with its declaration of independence, on May 14, 1948, the new nation inaugurated a chapter that simultaneously rejected and expanded on the foundations built since the Haskalah.

Two millennia after the Israelites were exiled after the capitulation of Jerusalem under the Roman army in 70 CE, their descendants, having kept, day after day, the holy city in their prayers, built a newly minted state, part of the large community of twentieth-century nations, just like them yet also unique in its foundation on Jewish values. Their longed-for homeland was now a reality.

(The term *Israelites* is generally used not for the first exile, but for the second.) At the heart of Zionism, a resourceful ideology capable of miraculously reinventing Jewish life as a whole, was the desire to have all the elements of a normal nation, including a shared mythology through literature and other means. That mythology needed to appear in the national language.

The theoretical founders of Zionism were rabbinical figures such as Zvi Hirsch Kalischer and Judah Alkalai and secular journalist, playwright, and short-story writer Theodor Herzl. A product of the Austro-Hungarian imperial culture—he was born in the eastern side of Budapest in 1860 and died at the age of forty-four in Reichenau an der Rax, in Austria, Herzl's manifesto *Der Judenstaat* (1896) was epochal for modern Jewish history. His utopian sci-fi novel, *Altneuland* (1902), which translates into *The Old New Land*, became a blueprint for reterritorializing Israel. It has a bad reputation, but it is much better than other utopian novels of its day. The novel's appearance in Hebrew the same year it was published in German has proved enduring in at least one way: the translation into Hebrew appeared under the clever title *Tel Aviv*. This might be among the very few cities that takes its name from literature. These two works by Herzl, both sorts of prophecy, contributed significantly to the foundation of the modern state of Israel. Herzl's work appeared in one of the most progressive intellectual Viennese newspapers of the day.

The other foundational Zionist figure whose literary output is important is Vladimir Jabotinsky. He wrote *Samson* (1927), a reimagining of the biblical story, which was made into the DeMille epic *Samson and Delilah* (1949), starring Heddy Lamar, although during the filming Hollywood dropped the militant Zionist subtext. Equally important is Jabotinsky's *The Five* (1936), a family saga that pulses with the life of Odessa and depicts the crises of the Jewish meeting with modernity. As a translator, his rendition into Russian of Chaim Nachman Bialik's *In the City of Slaughter* galvanized Jews under Czarist rule to rally around (his brand of) Zionism. And his translation into Hebrew of Poe's "The Raven" is still the standard and best translation of that classic. Jabotinsky delivered influential nationalist speeches ("Iron Wall"), produced a charming expansionist ditty ("Two Banks of the Jordan"), and was an enduring influence on Israeli politician Benjamin Netanyahu. Along the way, he published the first Hebrew atlas (1926), which did its best to create a narrative of reterritorialization to Zion—ironically, while Jabotinsky was in the diaspora.

A force behind creating a conduit through which the Zionist mythology could be presented was Lithuanian philologist and educator Eliezer ben Yehuda. His personal journey is a road map to understanding the foundation of the Jewish state and its literary tradition. Yiddish was ben Yehuda's first language, yet his early infatuation with Zionism made him perceive it as an unpleasant tongue that was embedded with an inferiority complex he believed to be ingrained in the diasporic mentality. As he himself recounted it, it was in his adolescence, when he borrowed a copy of Daniel Defoe's *Robinson Crusoe*, that he saw, metaphorically, the plight of Zionists before his eyes. He believed that to build a homeland, merely making *aliyah*, the Hebrew word for ascendance to the Promised Land, was insufficient. Those ready to commit needed to imagine themselves as new women and men in a number of ways. Ben Yehuda articulated his vision in his pamphlet, *The Burning Question* (1879), prompting Jews to imagine life in a new language. After a number of stops, he immigrated to Palestine. He was part of the first aliyah, which took place between 1882 and 1903, during which approximately twenty-five thousand to thirty-five thousand Jews came from the Pale and Yemen. He forbade his family from talking with neighbors in anything but Hebrew. He launched newspapers and dedicated himself to building a school system. And, in time, he embarked on producing the first dictionary of modern Hebrew.

Of that first aliyah, only about a fifth of the settlers stayed. A second aliyah occurred between 1905 and 1914 and it brought about thirty-five thousand Jews. This brought a generation of dreamers. The first crop of national writers, not yet Israelis, sprang from their experience of anti-Semitic outbursts in Europe. A commanding figure was Chaim Nachman Bialik, who did not make it to Palestine until 1924. He was a translator and editor, but especially a beloved poet in Yiddish and Hebrew—a year before his aliyah, his fiftieth birthday was celebrated with great fanfare in Berlin. Among the most important pieces Bialik wrote was a eulogy to the victims of the pogrom in Kishinev, in April 1903. He had been commissioned by the Jewish Historical Commission in Odessa, where he had moved, to travel to Kishinev to interview the victims. His epic poem *In the City of Slaughter* (1903) generated much debate in its denunciation of the passivity of Jews. Yet Bialik did not want to reject the legacy of eastern European Jews; on the contrary, he wanted to build the new nation on its cultural foundation. He celebrated the Talmud and other rabbinical literature as much-needed wisdom. With his friend Yehoshua Hana Ravnitzky, he edited an anthology called *Sefer ha-Haggadah* (1908–11), in which he compiled the folklore dating back to biblical times.

Other enthusiasts of the Hebrew renaissance were Shaul Tchernichovsky, a doctor and sonnet writer whose rhymed verses reinvigorated the language; Yosef Haim Brenner, part of a generation of pioneers that was eager to transform themselves into agricultural workers, but for whom work proved debilitating; Dvora Baron, among the first modern Hebrew women writers, whose distinct stories empathized with the weak and vulnerable; and Leah Goldberg, a lucid poet who also wrote children's books and taught at Hebrew University.

Of all the authors who moved to Palestine, either when it was under Ottoman rule or when it was under British mandate, Shmuel Yosef Halevi Czaczkes, a.k.a. Sh. Y. Agnon, gained international recognition. With his work translated into multiple languages, he shared the Nobel Prize for Literature with Nelly Sachs. Although he wrote in Yiddish as well, it is in Hebrew where Agnon shines. His language is allusive, melodic, and resonant in biblical imagery and echoes of Galicia, Germany, Jaffa, and Jerusalem, where he lived at the end of his life. His characters, feeling broken, are unified by a common thread: the search for internal fulfillment. Among Agnon's best works are *The Bridal*

Canopy (1931), a seriocomic episodic novel describing Galician Judaism in the nineteenth century through the prism of Reb Yudel, a poor but devout Jew wandering the countryside with his companion in search of bridegrooms for his three daughters; and *Shira* (1971), set in Jerusalem in the 1930s and 1940s, about a bored middle-aged professor searching for a nurse he met when his wife was giving birth to their third child. Agnon was convinced Hebrew was the language of Jewish memory. In it, the works of Jewish authors were stored for eternity.

In his travelogue, *To Jerusalem and Back* (1976), Saul Bellow described meeting Agnon one afternoon. They discussed an assortment of topics, including the masterpieces of Jewish literature. When Agnon said they would only survive in the sacred tongue, Bellow responded that, at the time of their dialogue, the majority of the Jews in the world communicated in English. He also mentioned that Jewish literature thrived in a panoply of tongues. And he mentioned Heinrich Heine. "Ah," Agnon sighed. "We have him safely translated into Hebrew." Like Bialik, Agnon was interested in diasporic rabbinical *responsa*. In this vein he produced *Days of Awe* (1938), a book of customs, interpretations, and legends for the Jewish days of mercy and forgiveness: Rosh Hashanah, Yom Kippur, and the days in between. He draws on an assortment of commentaries from the Torah, midrashic literature, the Talmud, and the prophets.

Zionism was built on three blind spots: the first is the outright rejection of the Jewish diaspora, a feeling that comes and goes depending on the character of those who nurture it; the second is the failure to recognize that, as an ideology, Zionism was an outgrowth of European nationalism; and the third was the refusal to recognize that the land targeted by the Zionists in the Middle East had a local population, the Palestinians. These three issues have defined Israel's relationship with its neighbors and the world at large. Each successive bloody cataclysm, from the War of Independence (1947–49), the Six-Day War (1967), the Yom

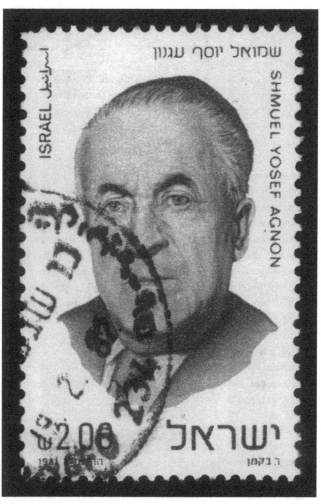

6. Israel honored S. Y. Agnon, the author of *The Bridal Canopy* and a master of the Hebrew language, with a postage stamp after he won the Nobel Prize for Literature. Agnon forged a literature about diaspora life in eastern Europe and its pioneering steps in the foundation of Israel as a modern Jewish state.

Kippur War (1973), the Lebanon War (1982), the first (1987–93) and second (2000–2005) intifadas, the second Lebanon war (2006), the Gaza War (2008), and onward brings along another national reckoning.

The transition between the early writers of modern Hebrew literature, responding to the anxiety of Jewish disappearance, and the later Israeli generation of writers, who respond to the constant wars for survival, is Ludwig Pfeuffer, a.k.a. Yehuda Amichai (the last name means "my people live"), considered Israel's national poet. An immigrant from Germany (he was a friend of Paul Celan and translated his work into Hebrew), Amichai also wrote novels, radio plays, and children's books. He used poetry like a biblical prophet to inquire into the soul of his nation.

Three writers, all born in Israel, also probed into the collective psyche, confronting its ghosts: A. B. Yehoshua, Amos Oz, and David Grossman. At times in his career, Yehoshua, a staunch nativist, looks at the Jewish diaspora as little more than a preparation for the arrival of the Jewish state. He once described European Jews as being able to change nationality like jackets: "Once they were Polish and Russian; now they are British and American." He, in contrast, only had one identity: "Being Israeli is my skin, not my jacket." His narratives always have a polyphonic style. Each of these voices comes from another segment in Israeli society. They address the challenges of, say, having an Arab become a normal member of a Jewish family, in *A Late Divorce* (1982), or in *Open Heart* (1994), running away from Israel to India in find one's true worth instead of staying in Israel.

Peace activist Amos Oz used his novels to engage with day-to-day encounters with day-to-day Israelis. Among his lasting contributions is the memoir *A Tale of Love and Darkness* (2002), about growing up in Jerusalem, a child of *olim*, meaning "ideological immigrants." David Grossman, a left-leaning intellectual whose son was killed in fighting between Israeli and

Hezbollah forces in Lebanon in 2006, in his novel *To the End of the Land* (2008), tells the story of a mother traversing the country from one end to another to avoid being at home, which is where she fears the military envoys will visit her to convey the news that one of her children has died in the war. By being away, she intrinsically believes she is able to live outside time. Grossman's journalism, featured in *The Yellow Wind* (1987) and *Sleeping on a Wire* (1992), delves into a topic that is unavoidable: Arabs in Israeli society. In conversations with an array of people, he questions the nation's ambivalence toward them.

That ambivalence might be seen, from the opposite perspective, in the work of Mizrahi writers like Sami Michael, who speaks Arabic and Hebrew, and whose novels, like *A Trumpet in the Wadi* (1987), explore the interface between European, Israeli, and Arab cultures. Another figure inhabiting this borderland is Anton Shammas, a Palestinian Israeli. Like the style of Agnon, to whom he is indebted, his genealogical novel *Arabesques* (1988), influenced by Gabriel García Márquez, tells the story of an extensive Arab family in Israel and beyond using a language with resonant biblical echoes. After its publication, Yehoshua and Shammas once engaged in a public dialogue about who owns modern Hebrew. Praising Shammas's style, Yehoshua said that his Palestinian foil was de facto borrowing a sacred language that Zionism had adapted into the modern world. It was, and would remain forever, the property of the Jews. Shammas disagreed. As an Israeli—he was born in Fassuta, south of the Lebanese border, and was a graduate of Hebrew University, he was a citizen—and therefore, the nation's language was his as well, no matter how intensely others wanted to portray him and other Palestinians using Hebrew as an impostor. The dialogue ended up pushing Shammas into exile. He moved to Ann Arbor, Michigan, where he became a professor of comparative literature.

Although Israel remains a macho culture, especially in the domains of politics and the military, Israeli literature, as in the case of its American Jewish variety, is a feast in terms of women's contributions. The shelf started with Baron and Goldberg and has expanded to include authors like novelist Amalia Kahana-Carmon, poet Dahlia Ravikovitch, Ronit Matalon, and Orly Castel-Bloom, the last two of Mizrahi descent. Matalon is a groundbreaking novelist; her feminist novel *And the Bride Closed the Door* (2016) is about a bride who on her wedding day shuts herself in a bedroom. And Castel-Bloom's *Human Parts* (2002) was a forerunner in tackling the issue of Palestinian suicide bombers. Both authors represent a trend in Israeli literature that awakened to the realities of the foundational Zionist dream.

Fragile at times, Israel in the twenty-first century remains the only democracy in its neighborhood. Literature is a fertile ground: there are more writers per capita in the country than almost anywhere else. And the number of readers is huge; in global polls, Israel contains far more readers than nations with similar population size. Yet ben Yehuda and the members of the first aliyah, it is fair to say, would have been shocked by how the language and its literature have evolved. Hebrew is heavily infused not only with Yiddish and Arabic, but also with Russian and, of course, English. Interested in new opportunities, or simply in response to global interests, thousands of Israelis have, in turn, themselves left the country—the antonym of aliyah is *yeridah*, "descent"—becoming, well, diaspora Jews again. This is, no doubt, another unlikely reversal. There are Israeli writers in the early twenty-first century who deliver their books in Hebrew, the way the Talmudists or Spanish poets did, yet they live in London or Los Angeles, preferring to see themselves as addressless. They are part of the ongoing ingathering of Jewish literature.

Chapter 7
The ingathering

In Hebrew, the word *kinnus* means "ingathering." In the introduction to the anthology of classical rabbinical literature, *Sefer Ha-Haggadah*, Chaim Nachman Bialik and Yehoshua Hana Ravnitzky, its editors, celebrated the concept of *aggadah*, storytelling, as "the classic expression of the spirit of the Jewish people." Everything one needs to know is ciphered in that literature. Bialik talked about "the ingathering," the capacity for the reader to wander, in an unimpeded way, in pursuit of myths through the various diasporas. Bialik had an even larger project in mind, though: to survey all literatures in the Jewish diaspora. He called it kinnus. Jewish storytelling, in this context, was miscellaneous in nature; it was, as I mentioned in the introduction, also centerless. This is all clear at the beginning of the twenty-first century: there are Jewish writers in almost every country on the globe. Their individual exploration fits into the national context while belonging to the larger aterritorial Jewish tradition.

Space allows me to concentrate on only a few examples. Some are connected to specific countries. Others are about the tension between the religious and secular worlds. One place to start is Argentina. At the end of the nineteenth century, as Jews were migrating to the United States, they sailed toward Buenos Aires. Theodor Herzl, in his disquisitions of Zionism, toyed with different possible locations for the Jewish state; Argentina was one of them. But it was not the hope to create a new Jewish homeland in the Pampas that attracted Yiddish-speaking dwellers. The reason was more practical: land was cheap in South America and the Argentinian government was intent on welcoming European immigrants (Italians, Russians, Jews), in the hope they would ultimately "civilize" a geography not densely populated.

The father of Latin American Jewish literature is Alberto Gerchunoff, who arrived from Russia as a little boy in one of the settlements specifically acquired by philanthropist Baron Maurice de Hirsch, whose mission it was to lift Jewish masses of the Pale out of poverty. He invested in resettling large numbers of people in *comunas* like Moisés Ville, villages that, in their organization, resembled the *shtetls* of the Old Country. In 1910, to celebrate the first centennial anniversary of Argentina's independence, Gerchunoff published a series of vignettes called *The Jewish Gauchos of the Pampas*. It is a lucid, lyrical exploration of life in the countryside. He had recently switched from Yiddish to Spanish. The book was a gift to his newly adopted homeland, which he described as *un país de advenimiento*, a land of advent. At the time, Argentina was indeed a promising new democracy that recently had overcome a tyrannical regime. Gerchunoff's view was idealistic: he believed the age of pogroms his family had experienced in Europe was being replaced by a new sense of freedom. Alas, the feeling was short-lived. In 1919, a violent outburst in Buenos Aires called *La Semana Trágica* ("the tragic week") that resembled a pogrom resulted in almost a hundred dead and scores of Jewish businesses destroyed. Coming to terms with the tragedy, Gerchunoff quickly became disillusioned. From that moment on, in his oeuvre he slowly embraced Zionism, discouraging other Jews from settling in Argentina.

The pathos displayed in his writing permeated many successive Jewish writers in that nation. A prime example is journalist Jacobo Timerman, the founder and editor of the newspaper *La Opinión*. As an advocate for human rights and freedom of the press, he antagonized the military junta that ruled Argentina in the seventies, in a period known as *Guerra sucia*, or Dirty War. He was arrested, imprisoned, and tortured. His ordeal is chronicled in his memoir, *Prisoner without a Name, Cell without a Number* (1981). Timerman shows the extent to which his oppressors used the language and techniques of the Nazis to extract information from him. On the other side of the spectrum, Marcos Aguinis, a physician and novelist, was secretary of culture under Raúl Alfonsín, Argentina's first democratically elected president after the military dictatorship. His novel *La gesta del marrano* (1991), known in English as *Against the Inquisition*, is about Francisco Maldonado da Silva, a physician in colonial times accused by the Holy Office of Judaizing and condemned as a heretic. Aguinis uses a historical figure as a surrogate to reflect on issues of freedom of speech and religion in the present.

Argentina is the only country in the Americas that witnessed not only a pogrom, but also an Iranian-orchestrated attack against the Buenos Aires Jewish community. It took place on July 18, 1994. The target was the Asociación Mutual Israelita Argentina, the city's Jewish community center. Around eighty-five people were killed and hundreds were wounded. That incident connected Latin American Jews with Middle Eastern politics. An exploration of the limits of assimilation and a defiance against systemic forms of hatred define the work of other Jewish writers from the region. A child of a mixed marriage between a Jewish immigrant father and an indigenous Quechua mother, Isaac Goldemberg, from Peru, delved into his existential dilemma in *The Fragmented Life of Don Jacobo Lerner* (1976). Like its author, the protagonist is consumed by trying to decide whether he is Peruvian or Jewish. Conversely, in *Death and the Maiden* (1990), the Chilean playwright Ariel Dorfman built a tight plot around a woman who, after recognizing the fascist regime's prison doctor during the tyranny of General Augusto Pinochet who once raped her in prison, must decide whether to seek revenge. She identifies him coincidentally when her husband brings him home. Chile is not identified by Dorfman as the country where the action occurs, nor is Pinochet named as the tyrant.

These works are a barometer of the status of Jews in the Spanish-speaking world. Do they live as pariahs? Are they fully accepted? Similar questions are asked in Brazil, the largest, most diverse Latin American country. Clarice Lispector, who wrote in Portuguese even though her first languages were Ukrainian and Yiddish, was a modernist whose style resembled—actually, it improved—that of Virginia Woolf. The author of about a dozen novels, multiple stories, essays, and newspaper columns, her Jewishness, as in Kafka, does not manifest itself overtly, yet it is palpable as a sensibility in every page. Lispector's most "Jewish" novel is *The Hour of the Star* (1977), in which the tragic odyssey of an indigent woman, called Macabea (after the Maccabees), in search of a place for herself in the world, ends abruptly. The narrator's condescending comments make Macabea even more vulnerable. Lispector seems to be meditating on the resistance of Brazilian culture to embrace individuals on their own terms, a topic at the heart of the question on the region's Jewish assimilation.

The most multifaceted of all Latin American Jewish writers, Moacyr Scliar, produced an oeuvre full of humor. He wrote myriad novels, hundreds of stories, children's and young adult literature, studies on humor, travelogues, memoirs, dictionaries, and cookbooks. His work was adapted to film and radio. A descendent of Yiddish-speaking immigrants to Porto Alegre, in Rio Grande do Sul, he was a physician by training but spent much of his time writing. In *The Strange Nation of Rafael Mendes* (1987), he delves into the search by a Christian business for his Jewish ancestry dating back to Brazil's colonial period. Another of Scliar's books, *The Majesty of Xangu* (1997), features a doctor who abandons his career in the city to become a full member of an aboriginal tribe in the Brazilian Amazon. In another, *The Woman Who Wrote the Bible* (1999), Scliar develops, in fictional terms, the theory by

7. **Moacyr Scliar at his desk in his home in Porto Alegre, 1988. Internationally acclaimed physician and novelist, Scliar, the author of *The Centaur in the Garden*, used humor to reflect on Jewish life in Brazilian society.**

Harold Bloom that the Hebrew bible was written by a female author in King David's court.

Scliar's most famous book is the Kafkaesque novel *The Centaur in the Garden* (1980). The protagonist, Guedali Tartakovsky, whom the reader first meets during a celebration in honor of his thirty-eighth birthday, is a centaur—half horse, half human—who is Jewish to boot. He longs to find a Jewish centauress to accompany him. His plight oscillates between societal alienation and personal fulfillment. At one point late in the narrative, the protagonist chooses to undergo surgery to make him fully human. Yet that does not make him happy either. The message of Scliar's allegory is clear: uniqueness is both a burden and a gift. Delivered in an unadorned style Scliar perfected throughout his career, the novel might be read as the Latin American response to Kafka's *The Metamorphosis*. There are also echoes of Sholem Aleichem in the use of social comedy—never irreverent, always gentle—as a strategy to overcome alienation.

Half a world away, South Africa has been a fertile ground for Jewish literature. Nadine Gordimer, the recipient of the Nobel Prize in 1991, used her terse, politically engaged writing to explore the volatile racial relations of Blacks and Whites during Apartheid. Although, like Lispector, she does not tackle Jewish themes frontally, in novels like *Burger's Daughter* (1979) she tried to look at her country's history from the intimacy of those who experienced it. It is the story of a woman, the daughter of a martyred opponent to Apartheid, trying to come to terms with her father's legacy. This particular one is a thinly veiled homage to Bram Fischer, a lawyer of Afrikaans descent who was imprisoned for his political activities.

On a somewhat different route, Dan Jacobson, a descendant of Lithuanian immigrants to Johannesburg, who lived in London most of his career, used his writing to explore his roots. He is best known for his story "The Zulu and the Zayda" (1959), an affecting exploration of empathy between a Black man in a country ruled by Whites and a Jewish immigrant. Unfortunately, the story is seldom read outside South Africa, and even there it has fallen somewhat into oblivion. Their exchange leads to an discussion on tolerance and a dismantling of stereotypes. It became a Broadway musical in 1965. Jacobson delved into biblical stories in novels like *The Rape of Tamar* (1970). And his memoir *Hershel's Kingdom* (1998) used a number of objects he inherited from his Lithuanian grandfather, a rabbi, as touchstones to trace his path from Europe to South Africa and back. It is a lucid example of diasporic Jewish writing: one is never of one place only, yet nowhere is one more comfortable than in one's place.

One of the foundational Jewish voices in the diaspora is from Britain: Israel Zangwill, a nineteenth-century cultural Zionist close to Theodor Herzl. Zangwill was not only quite likely the most famous Jew in the Western world; he was also the most read Jewish writer in the English language until sometime probably in the mid-twentieth century. His *Children of the Ghetto: A Study of a Peculiar People* (1892) put the very term *ghetto* into popular usage in English. The collection was a bestseller and altered the landscape of British literature in the late Victorian era. Likewise, his *Dreamers of the Ghetto* (and other "ghetto" volumes) proved very popular. He also wrote the first locked-room murder mystery (*Big Bow Mystery* [1882]), which spawned everything the very non-Jewish Agatha Christie ever wrote. Then there was his play *The Melting Pot* (1909), which premiered in Washington, DC, with Theodore Roosevelt in attendance and which popularized (and possibly coined) the phrase by which America understands its assimilatory culture. And if all that is not enough, he was the man who first got Herzl's ideas for a Jewish state in print (an excerpt in English) and introduced Herzl to sympathetic supporters in late nineteenth-century London. Plus, Zangwill translated many of the medieval Hebrew poets who later made their way into English synagogue liturgy. Likewise, as publisher and distributer of a newspaper throughout Czarist Russia that explained how to immigrate to the United States, he was responsible for helping untold thousands of Jews escape to Europe and America, where he worked with Jacob Schiff on the Galveston Plan that helped distribute about ten thousand Jewish immigrants to Texas and the West Coast states. Unquestionably, Zangwill is at the heart of diasporism.

Britain has remained a fertile ground for Jewish literature. Harold Pinter, a Nobel Prize–winning playwright, screenwriter, and actor known for his left-wing political engagement and his critique of power, does not feature overt Jewish themes in plays like *The Birthday Party* (1957), *The Homecoming* (1964), and *Betrayal* (1978). Yet the Jewish sensibility is tangible in the way he tackled relationships. Pinter also adapted into film Kafka's *The Trial* (1993). And Howard Jacobson, in novels like *The Finkler Question* (2010), uses acerbic comedy in novels to delve into questions of British Jewish identity. One of them, *Shylock Is My Name* (2016), is a modern reimagining of Shakespeare's protagonist in *The*

Merchant of Venice, frequently described as one of the most anti-Semitic characters in world literature.

Here, I give a few other remarks on Russian Jewish literature, which reflects, succinctly, on the Soviet approach to Yiddish. The war against freedom of faith and expression was relentless. Boris Pasternak, author of *Doctor Zhivago* (1957), who was raised by an assimilated Jewish family and expressed little interest in his heritage, was punished for his political dissidence. Pasternak was awarded the Nobel Prize, but the Soviets forced him to turn it down. The turbulence of the Stalin years is palpable in the work of Vasily Grossman. Born in a part of Ukraine that was then Russia, he was a journalist who lived in the Soviet Union. During a period of his life, he endorsed Stalinism. His book *For a Just Cause* (1952) was mostly ideological propaganda. Grossman then made a U-turn, delivering a sequel called *Life and Fate* (1980), a largely autobiographical, multicharacter novel that takes place in 1942–43 and is about the plight of the protagonist, Viktor Shtrum, and his Jewish family.

While the Stalinist oppressiveness abated somewhat after the dictator's death in 1953, the atmosphere of fear remained. Joseph Brodsky, a Russian poet, was born in Leningrad (now St. Petersburg), was mentored by Anna Akhmatova, and was among the most celebrated exiled anti-Soviet voices. He established as his ancestor Joseph ben Isaac Bekhor Shor, a twelfth-century French Talmudist and poet. Known for his sharp intelligence, delicate sensibility, and polyglot talent, Brodsky, an only child, published a variety of apolitical poems like "Pilgrims" and "The Jewish Cemetery near Leningrad" in underground Russian magazines such as *Sintaksis* that were judged to be examples of a bourgeois aesthetic (he was deemed "pornographic" and "anti-Soviet" by the authorities). In his essay "Less Than One" (1986), Brodsky reflected on the dim living conditions he and his parents endured when he was a child. Still, his bookishness and the recognition of poetry as an escape offered him a palliative retreat. He was put on trial and deemed a "parasite." Brodsky was sentenced to five years of hard labor (he served eighteen months) on a farm in the village of Norenskaya, in the Archangelsk region, 350 miles from Leningrad. Protests from Russian writers such as Yevgeny Evtushenko and Akhmatova, as well as from Westerners such as Jean-Paul Sartre, turned him into a cause célèbre. With the help of W. H. Auden and others, he was allowed to go into exile. He taught at the University of Michigan and Mount Holyoke College. He was awarded the Nobel Prize in 1987.

Before the fall of the Berlin Wall in 1989, and of the Soviet Union in 1991, there was already an exodus of Russian Jews. This departure was intensified once state-wide control disappeared. Thousands immigrated freely to Israel, the United States, and Canada. For the most part, they had advanced degrees and came from a variety of professions. Years later, it was not surprising that a crop of Russia-born writers, or their children, flourished in Hebrew and English. Their literature infused new air into Jewish literature. One example is Dina Rubina, born in Tashkent, Uzbekistan, who immigrated to Israel at the age of thirty-three. Her novel *Petrushka's Syndrome* (2010) is about the interplay of Russian and Israeli cultures. And Gary Shteyngart, born also in St. Petersburg, arrived in America at the age of seven. His novels, including the dystopian *Abusrdistan* (2006), are characterized by a slapstick, hyperkinetic style.

Other lands have been equally fertile. In France, Jewish writers like Irène Némirovsky, Romain Gary, Georges Perec, and Nobel Prize winner Patrick Modiano have produced influential work. Perec, a descendant of Yiddish writer I. J. Peretz, was one of the most enchanting twentieth-century experimental writers, as well as a filmmaker and documentalist. His father died in the Holocaust. He was a member of the group Ouvroir de littérature potentielle, which sought to create literature out of mathematical problems as well as some quasi-random methods like a game of chess or Tarot cards. *A Void* (1969) is a lipogrammatic novel written without the letter *e*. And his novel *Life: A User's Manual* (1978) looks at the interconnected lives of the inhabitants of 11 rue Simon-Crubellier, a fictitious Parisian apartment block. As for Modiano, in novels like *The Search Warrant* (2000) and *In the Café of Lost Youth* (2016), he looks at the ways the past defines the present.

The same goes for Canada, with A. M. Klein, a lawyer and poet who, with his novella *The Second Scroll* (1951), set the foundation for Canadian Jewish culture. Mordecai Richler was a journalist and comic humorist. His novels, including *The Apprenticeship of Duddy Kravitz* (1959), explored ambivalence as a feature of Jewish life. In Italy, authors such as Italo Svevo, Giorgio Bassani, and Natalia Ginzburg delved into Jewish life in various corners of the country. Svevo (his real name was Aron Ettore Schmitz) was a businessman from Trieste who wrote short stories, novels, and plays and was a close friend of James Joyce. His novel *Confessions of Zeno* (1923) is shaped as a memoir about a family written at the insistence of the narrator's psychiatrist. Bassani, in narratives like *The Garden of Finzi-Continis* (1977), explored the life of Italian Jews of Sephardic descent in the region of Ferrara. And Ginzburg, a member of Italy's Communist Party, wrote intimate essays and novels like *Family Lexicon* (2017) about assimilated Jews in Rome under the fascist regime during and after the Second World War.

Finally, a major theme in twenty-first-century diaspora literature is the renunciation of ultra-Orthodox practices by those who grew up in a tightly knit religious milieu. Scores of memoirs, mostly written by women from various Hasidic sects like the Satmar in Williamsburg, Brooklyn, recount the ordeal of survival and the onslaught of shame, guilt, and regret experienced as they entered the secular world. One example is Deborah Feldman's autobiography, *Unorthodox: The Scandalous Rejection of My Hasidic Roots* (2012), about her flight, in response to a failed marriage, to Berlin, where her divorced mother lived. Feldman's piece was made into a Netflix series. These narratives are published in Israel and America. Intriguingly, these themes echo the tension between Hasidim and representatives of the Haskalah in the eighteenth century.

All these examples are evidence of the ingathering Bialik referred to in his introduction to *Sefer ha-Hagadah*, except that from the second half of the twentieth century onward, with the decentralization of Jewish culture and the easy and fast access to the printing processes, their spread became truly global.

Chapter 8
The critic's "I"

German Marxist critic Walter Benjamin, author of the seminal essay "The Work of Art in the Age of Mechanical Reproduction" (1935), once imagined bringing out a book composed exclusively of anonymous quotations from other authors. It would be organized in such way as to make a case about how our universe is but a scrapbook in need of interpretation. Although Benjamin never completed the task, the idea behind it is perfect to reflect on what literary criticism—in particular, Jewish criticism—does.

There is no literature without critical appraisal. Every reader interprets; that is, every reader experiences a critical reaction. Yet not every reader is a critic. A critic is a lifelong reader whose task is to connect interpretations. Writers need critics as much as critics need writers, to the point that one without the other feels like an orphan. This is especially clear in the Jewish literary tradition, famous for what might be called *pairings*: Meir Weiner and Dan Miron on Sholem Aleichem, Walter Benjamin and Hannah Arendt on Franz Kafka, Lionel Trilling on Isaac Babel, and so on. The gift of a certain author suddenly seems neater, more focused, thanks to a critic's discerning eye. And the reverse is also true: an author's universe sharpens the critic's talents, opening up new vistas into whole aspects of culture.

Among *Am ha-Sefer*, the critic occupies a special position in Jewish life: she is a reader's reader. Not a few writers dislike critics because they do not want to be criticized. Conversely, critics might also nurture a distaste for certain authors, finding them defensive, allergic to outside views. Yet even these authors would agree that criticism is essential to understanding the place of literature in society. The roots of Jewish critical thinking are in rabbinical disquisition. Numerous passages of the Talmud might be described as exercises in biblical criticism. A Tanaite commentator might disagree with his Amorite counterpart on how to understand the episode of Jacob's ladder in Genesis 28:10–17. It is not about finding a common ground; their disagreement is the purpose. After all, it is interpretation that makes the universe meaningful.

Yet among Jews, the critic's role as a clearly defined profession only comes about with the Haskalah because of the new conception of belles lettres. As literature becomes a favorite pastime, so does the dissemination of its power. In the second half of the nineteenth century, Jews find themselves in heated discussions in European cafés as well as in newspapers, magazines, forewords, interviews, and other printed material. Among the earliest practitioners is Heinrich Heine, an accomplished lyrical poet who was born into a Jewish family but converted to Lutheranism in his late twenties and was never a believer. An assiduous traveler, he moved to Paris, where he was a correspondent for *Allgemeine Zeitung*. Although he was ambivalent about his Jewishness, Heine wrote reviews, essays, memoirs, novels—such as *The Rabbi of Bacherach* (1840)—and meditations of various aspects of the Bible, aside from the *Junge Leiden* for which he is justifiably remembered.

Yiddish literature cannot be conceived with its titanic critics. Some writers like Sholem Aleichem produced valuable pieces of criticism. Among them is his article "*A briv tsu a gutn fraynd*" (A letter to a close friend), which appears as an afterword to his novel *Stempenyu* (1888), in which he presents himself, along with Mendele Mokher Sforim and Itzkhok Leib Peretz, as a literary triumvirate, thus creating an aesthetic dialogue between generations. In countless ways, the afterword served to anchor the Yiddish literary tradition in the eyes of readers, who from that moment on could understand their writers as sages with an ultimate purpose. And literary criticism served as a crucial benchmark for successive writers. Itzkhok Leib Peretz was the publisher of *Yontev Bletekh* (Holiday pages), which argued for enlightenment and socialist ideals. He edited *Di Yidishe Bibliotek* (The Jewish library), which published a wide array of articles on secular subjects, including science. Writing in both Hebrew and Yiddish, he became a literary and intellectual magnet for younger Yiddish writers, many of whom later became well known (for example, David Pinski, Abraham Reisen, Sholem Asch, and Joseph Opatoshu).

Two Yiddish critics developed an oeuvre of categorical importance. One was the neurologist Israel Isidor Elyashev, a.k.a. Ba'al Makhshoves, which means "master of thought," a sharp, incisive commentator whose collected articles (*Geklibene shrift*, 1910), believed to be the breakthrough volume of literary criticism in Yiddish, push for a more complex understanding of literature rather than the merely pedagogical, which was the stand of earlier practitioners up until Mendele Mokher Sforim. A Zionist (he participated as a delegate from Germany in the First Zionist Congress, in Basel, Switzerland, in 1897), he was a passionate reader of everything Yiddish, believing it to be "folk" literature. Among the intellectual quests Ba'al Makhshoves embraced was the distinction, in the popular imagination, between Yiddish and Hebrew: What place did each occupy? Did they constitute two different literary traditions? In 1918, during an important writer's conference in Bukovina, Romania, he argued in favor of seeing Ashkenazic civilization as having two languages and a dozen echoes from other foreign languages, yet only one literature, meaning that, in his view, Jewish literature needed to be seen as a single polyglot current.

The second critic was Shmuel Charney, a.k.a. Shmuel Niger, who was interested in the social and ideological sides of literature. One of his interests was Peretz, whom he believed to be the centripetal force of the Yiddish literary canon, although later in life he placed greater attention on Sholem Aleichem's oeuvre. He edited important journals, the most significant of which was, while still in Vilna, *Literarishe Monatshriftn* (*Literary Monthly Journal*), widely credited with having launched the Yiddish literary renaissance. Charney also worked for a number of newspapers, including a handful he was involved in after his immigration to the United States in 1919. He is credited for launching a study of Yiddish literature from multiple perspectives. For instance, he was in charge of *Der Pinkes* (*The Record Book*, 1913), a sophisticated enterprise that studied language and folklore and featured substantial bibliographical references.

Another important Yiddish literary critic, better known as an educator, was Argentina's Samuel Rollansky. He edited a one-hundred-volume anthology known as *Musteverk*, in which he distilled what in his view were the essential components of the sprawling Yiddish literature across the countless diasporas, from Europe to the United States and the Spanish—and Portuguese-speaking—Americas, South Africa, Australia, and other places. The sheer ambition of the endeavor is stunning: it pays tribute to the polyphonic nature of a literary tradition that, in over a hundred years, had become world-class.

In Hebrew, the critical work of Perets Smolenskin is of foundational importance. While he wrote a series of novels, it was as editor of the monthly *Ha-Shahar* (The dawn) where his literary and political ideas—he was a fervent Zionist—crystallized. The criticism that Smolenskin and others engaged in was influenced by European trends and was often positivist in its approach. It not only sought to understand a work of art in its historical context but also pondered what its use was. Did it advance Zionist, Socialist, Communist, or any other ideological causes? The first and second aliyahs changed the nature of Hebrew literary criticism. A figure useful for understanding this change is historian and literary scholar Yoseph Klausner. The redactor of the *Encyclopedia Hebraica*, an important reference project that brought together knowledge around the centralizing idea of Hebrew, he wrote *A History of Modern Hebrew Literature: 1785–1930* (1932).

Russia too was a cradle of Jewish literary critics and theorists. Among the significant ones was Yury Nikolaevich Tynyanov, an authority on Pushkin. Tynyanov collaborated with perhaps the most important Jewish literary scholar, Roman Jakobson, famous for his contributions to semantics and semiotics. Together they wrote *Theses on Language* (1928), in which they established structural laws pertaining to literature that years later would influence another important Jewish anthropologist and semiotician, Claude Lévi-Strauss. For instance, they argued that a scientific study of literature, with an accurate terminology, would distinguish literature as a hierarchical organization with its own rules and regulations.

In large part, the path of the modern Jewish critic as a semiotician was opened by Walter Benjamin himself. Although he was far from being either the first or the most accepted in Weimar Germany, his originality and shrewdness, manifested in reviews in literary supplements, essays in journals, and radio programs that could be seen as forerunners of the podcast, left a lasting impact. He was interested in popular culture—he wrote about Mickey Mouse—when few others were, looked at photography and fingerprints as police procedures, and reflected, prophetically, on technological reproduction as an integral part of twentieth-century art. His unfinished work, *The Arcade Project* (1927–40), was an attempt to understand, in multifarious ways, the cultural role of shopping arcades. He also wrote a seminal early work on why Franz Kafka mattered. Benjamin belongs to the so-called Frankfurt School, a gathering of social theorists composed of critics, academics, and political dissidents with a distinctive Marxist (e.g., anticapitalist) approach coalesced at the Institute of Social Research of Frankfurt's Goethe University in the years between the end of the First World War and the ascendance of Hitler to power in Germany. Passionate, yet ambivalent about his own Jewishness, Benjamin meditated about it profusely with his close friend Gershom Scholem. They kept a correspondence that in itself is a worthy critical document.

In Russia, the formalists were led by Roman Jakobson, Boris Eichenbaum, and Viktor Shklovsky. This school argued for a scientific study of literature and, more specifically, poetic language. They rejected the view that literature is a statement of the history, politics, and culture of a nation and that it is a prism whereby to appreciate an author's opinions. Jakobson focused on phonology, morphology, syntax, and semantics. He was fascinated by the shared grammatical structures of languages and by the general features pertaining to all global languages. Through figures like the French Jewish anthropologist Claude Lévi-Strauss, he was instrumental in the shaping of structuralism. His diverse contributions include the essay "On the Linguistic Aspects of Translation" (1959). Along with Shklovsky, Eichenbaum was a member of the Obščestvo Ilzučenija Poètičeskogo Jazyka, known for its acronym OPOJAZ, the Society for the Study of Poetic Language. Founded in St. Petersburg in 1916, it was a group devoted to the analysis of literary semiotics. Eichenbaum wrote a trilogy on Leo Tolstoy as well as on Pushkin, Gogol, Akhmatova, and Lermontov. For his part, Shklovsky was a theorist—he is the author of *Theory of Prose* (1925)—as well as a novelist, screenwriter (he wrote the script of *Jews on Land* [1927]), and memoirist. He wrote on Maxim Gorsky, Tolstoy, Vladimir Mayakovsky, and Laurence Sterne. He was interested in how plot is built and was among the first critics to write insightfully about film. Shklovsky believed that in art the artifact itself is unimportant; what matters is the creative process.

Literary criticism sprang up in a particularly vigorous way among the descendants of Jewish immigrants in the United States. New York by then had become the new center of Jewish culture. A cadre of loosely connected Jewish intellectuals, including Lionel Trilling, Delmore Schwartz, Alfred Kazin, and Irving Howe, shaped artistic and ideological tastes, at times from a Trotskyite perspective, at others from a neoliberal point of view, and occasionally sliding from one end of the spectrum to the other in the second half of the twentieth century. They accomplish the task from a variety of pulpits. Trilling was the first Jewish professor to receive tenure at Columbia's English Department. Schwartz wrote celebrated short stories, particularly "In Dreams Begin Responsibility," a psychoanalytical exploration of his own upbringing as imagined on a movie screen. Kazin explored American literature and wrote *A Walker in the City* (1951), detailing his childhood and adolescence in the Brownsville section of Brooklyn. Subsequent memoirs traced his journey into Manhattan and onto the New York mainstream. And Howe devoted years to researching *World of Our Fathers: The Journey of the East European Jews to America and the Life They Found and Made* (1976), which offered a context to the journey of Jewish immigrants to America. He wrote another memoir, *A Margin of Hope* (1982), in which he described his political education and the relationships he built as a Jew with the New York intellectual establishment as well as with European writers in France, England, Germany, and elsewhere.

One of Howe's seldom explored facets is his role as editor. Like Charney and other Yiddish predecessors, in 1954 he cofounded a journal, *Dissent*, devoted to politics and culture. And he had a hand in shaping a slew of anthologies. He edited, sometimes with a collaborator, approximately two dozen, from compendiums dedicated to Yiddish stories to others on Yiddish poetry, Soviet

Jewry, and *The Best of Sholem Aleichem* (1979); and in the realm of non-Jewish themes, he oversaw volumes on Leo Tolstoy, Rudyard Kipling, and George Orwell. An editor is a curator, an enabler, and a savvy reader. These talents are clear in Howe's anthology *A Treasury of Yiddish Stories* (1954), coedited with Yiddishist Eliezer Greenberg. Released not fifteen years after the end of the Second World War, this volume was one of the first times American audiences, and Jews in particular, had an opportunity to appreciate the world destroyed by the Nazis as portrayed by its own writers. The contents included contributions from Itzkhok Leib Peretz, Sholem Asch, Abraham Reisen, and Isaac Bashevis Singer. The piece by Singer, "Gimpel the Fool," suggested to Howe by Greenberg, was translated by Saul Bellow. It not only became one of the most important short stories in Yiddish literature, but also acquired the status of classic worldwide. As mentioned before, it also catapulted Singer's career.

Although there is plenty of Jewish literary criticism in university circles, the style is often trite and the quality stilted and uninspiring. An exception, not necessarily for the right reasons, is Brooklyn-born Yale professor Harold Bloom. From his academic pulpit, he pontificated about the importance of literature in a world increasingly uninterested in ideas. He wrote profusely on Shakespeare, who he said had created our understanding of what it means to be human, and about British and American poets such as John Milton, John Donne, William Blake, Walt Whitman, and Emily Dickinson. Bloom developed a theory, known as "the anxiety of influence," which suggests that all writers steal, consciously and otherwise, from their predecessors. The act of borrowing is then repressed, or, in Bloom's own terms, "revised" in one way or another by the new generation's poet. It is a theory clearly rooted in the conception, at the base of Judaism, that we are in conversation not only with our contemporaries, but also with those who came before us and those who will come after. A Yiddish speaker, Bloom was known to have a prodigious mind and an almost superhuman memory. Able to read at an astonishingly fast speed and photographically remember entire poems and plays, he also wrote about Jewish subjects, for instance, Kabbalah. He was particularly attracted to biblical narrative. At one point, he proposed the idea—discredited by scholars—that a woman wrote portions of the Torah.

The second half of the twentieth century witnessed a veritable explosion of female public Jewish intellectuals, a response to the dramatic changes taking place in the culture in terms of women's rights. Among the sharpest was American poet Adrienne Rich. A feminist, she wrote superb essays about the writer's political commitment, the need to develop a female "glance" to appreciate works of literature, and the urgency with which writers, regardless of gender, need to speak up to power. Her best essays are collected in *Blood, Bread, and Poetry: Selected Prose, 1979-1985* (1986). On the opposite side of the ideological spectrum is Cynthia Ozick, who, aside from her baroque, Henry James–inspired novels about Bruno Schulz and other Jewish topics, was an assiduous essayist. Her nonfiction is included in four volumes, among them *Metaphor & Memory* (1989) and *Quarrel and Quandary* (2000). Ideologically conservative, Ozick for the most part concentrated on nonpolitical topics, except when it comes to the concert of critical voices attacking the policies of Israel toward Palestinians, which she opposed. One such example was her public debate, in the late 1980s, with Palestinian novelist Anton Shammas on the Hebrew language. Shammas argued that Hebrew, the language of a cosmopolitan modern state, no longer belonged exclusively to the Jewish people but to everyone in the nation, including Palestinians, Filipinos, Romanians, Somalis, and other non-Jewish immigrants. Ozick adamantly rejected the idea. In her view, Hebrew, by virtue of its origins, would always belong to the Jews.

In terms of generation, Susan Sontag, née Susan Rosenblatt, though younger, also belongs to the cadre of New York Jewish intellectuals. Yet she is as much a byproduct of that milieu as she

is a cosmopolitan whose interests redefined an entire era.
A novelist, playwright, theater director, and overall culture
commentator with a meticulously crafted, contrarian style, Sontag
took upon herself the question of what it is that our minds do
when we interpret. We insist on dispensing judgment on what we
see, but that judgment ends up sabotaging our relationship with
others. She also explored the role of photography in modern
times, how illness was generally understood in the twentieth
century, and how we react when we see others in pain. In books
like *Styles of Radical Will* (1969), *On Photography* (1977), and
Illness as Metaphor (1978), Sontag was closer to the French model
of *intellectuelle* than to her American counterparts.

Sontag believed that literature enlarges our sense of human
possibility. It is a window not only to the outside but also—and
especially—to what she called "inwardness." Having married the
sociologist and cultural critic Philip Rieff and had a son, she had a
number of relationships with women, including photographer
Annie Leibovitz. However, she kept her bisexuality secret. She was
also a cancer survivor. One of her most penetrating books, one
with unavoidable Jewish connotations, is *Regarding the Pain of
Others* (2003). In it she looks at the devastations of war, from the
lynchings of Blacks in the American South to the Nazi atrocities to
Vietnam, Rwanda, and Israel, whose policies toward the
Palestinians she was critical of. She argues that our view of
suffering as well as "the pain of others" is rooted in religious
thinking. Sontag links pain to sacrifice and sacrifice to exaltation.
She reflects on how suffering, when seen through the prism of a
modern sensibility, "is a mistake or an accident or a crime . . . ,
something that makes one feel powerless."

On the surface, there is not much that is Jewish in her perspective.
Yet as soon as one submerges deeply in her work, it becomes clear
that she is in dialogue with an ancient rabbinical tradition of
relentlessly questioning everything around us. She seeks meaning
in silence and perplexity. In that sense, the critic, by activating a

Sonta*g*

Essays of the 1960s & 70s

Against Interpretation
Styles of Radical Will
On Photography
Illness as Metaphor
Uncollected Essays

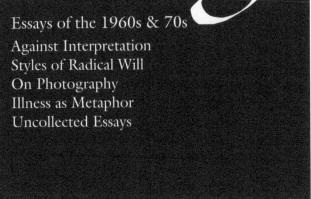

8. Susan Sontag, the grande dame of American intellectual life in
the second half of the twentieth century, used a sharp Jewish sensibility
to explore, in stylized essays, a variety of topics, from the role of
photography in contemporary culture to how suffering has been
understood throughout history.

sensibility triggered by close reading, completes the task of literature: to become a dialogue.

In the age of social media, literary criticism descends into shameless advertising. The capacity to read closely, to ponder contradicting ideas, and to sustain an argument is dramatically curtailed. Indeed, social media, in its engagement, is defined by distraction: it requires the user to nervously jump from one theme to another with little by way of connection. In such an ecosystem the act of criticism is easily understood as destructive rather than constructive. As a result, reading books, and doing so by keeping a steady literary diet, is the domain of the small educated elite whose interests do not align only with ephemeral cultural fashion. The truth is, this trend, while looking new, has been consistent since the Enlightenment: reading is an activity that, while aspiring to be democratic, is reserved for the very few. Still, the need to interpret—for example, to find meaning—in what is read remains a Jewish compulsion.

Chapter 9
Translation matters

A salient feature in Jewish literary history is its translational drive. As a result of the aterritorial quality of Jewish life, almost from the first moment books are made available, translation into an assortment of languages has become the norm.

Translators are bridges across cultures. It is not surprising how central the act of translation is in Jewish life. To translate is to interpret, to reinvent a text in a different language. Translators are close readers—maybe the closest reader an author ever gets. The activity is in the Torah from the outset. In Genesis 1:1–4, the divine wishes to create the world are translated into words: "1: In the beginning God created the heaven and the earth. 2: And the earth was without form, and void; and darkness was upon the face of the deep. And the Spirit of God moved upon the face of the waters. 3: And God said, Let there be light: and there was light. 4: And God saw the light, that it was good: and God divided the light from the darkness." As a result, in *Sefer ha-Zohar*, one of the cornerstones of Kabbalah, the statement is made that language already existed before Creation. There are also the dual concepts of *lashon ha-kodesh*, the divine language, a nonverbal code in which God communicates with Itself, and *lashon b'nei adam*, the human language, the language God uses to communicate with humans and that humans use to communicate with themselves.

And there is the foundational legend of the Tower of Babel, in Genesis 11:1–9, which serves as a central myth about the tension between the universal language humans supposedly spoke at the beginning and a plurality of human tongues, which derive from divine punishment for the hubris that humans evidence in building a structure capable of reaching heaven. In the Babel legend, which has its roots in ancient civilizations like Sumeria (a similar story is told in *Enmerkar and the Lord of Aratta*, a legendary account dating back to around the twenty-first century BC), a ziggurat, a massive structure common in Mesopotamia, is built in the land of Shinar by the people to reach heaven. The assumption is that humans are presumptuous, tempting divine authority. The hubris is punished by multiplying the number of languages so that humans will be doomed not to understand each other.

Reflection on our post–Tower of Babel punishment abounds in Jewish literature. Some in the Talmud and beyond do not see it as a punishment at all, but as an opportunity for diversity: the more human languages, the more cultural variety. Walter Benjamin, in his essay "The Task of the Translator," proposes translation not as a subservient, anonymous effort but as a form of art. Likewise, in his book *After Babel* (1975), French-born American literary critic George Steiner, who wrote in English, French, and German (this volume was written in English), delves into the question of translation as essential to human interaction. "To understand is to decipher," Steiner posited, "and to hear significance is to translate." And Jacques Derrida, bridging the challenges posed by a polyglot life, stated, "We only ever speak one language. We never speak only one language."

Three Jewish philosophers reflected on language as well: Ludwig Wittgenstein, an Austrian of Ashkenazi descent who settled in Cambridge, England believed that everything might be reduced to language and that the limits of our language are the limits of our world ("*whereof* one cannot speak, thereof one must be silent");

Emmanuel Levinas, who was Lithuanian and lived in France, explored how human language is a veil through which we reveal or hide others ("the more I return to myself, the more I divest myself"); and Derrida, a literary theorist of Mizrahi descent who also lived in Paris and wrote in French, in what he called "grammatology," suggested, appropriately, that how we build sentences is how we interpret our world ("the writer writes *in* a language and *in* a logic whose proper system, laws, and life his discourse by definition cannot dominate absolutely"). Indeed, Jewish literature is, at its core, about language. This means that the various genres—poetry, fiction, essay, theater, memoir—are linguistically playful. Yosef Haim Brenner, an experimental Hebrew novelist before Israel became an independent state, mixed Hebrew, Yiddish, Aramaic, English, and Arabic. And in Henry Roth's *Call It Sleep*, David Schearl, the protagonist, communicates in a type of Yinglish—a mix of Yiddish and English—that Roth recreates through fractured grammar.

These and other linguistic mediations are at the heart of how Jews relate to God, nature, and society. One of the features of Jewish life is its polyglotism. More than most people, Jews are known for being conversant in multiple languages. This, obviously, is conducive to translation in general. Jewish authors are frequently also translators: Heinrich Heine translated the medieval Hebrew poets Shmuel Hanagid, Shlomo ibn Gabirol, Moses ibn Ezra, and Judah Halevi into German. Emma Lazarus translated Heine's German versions into English. Contemporary examples include Hebrew poets Nathan Alterman and Leah Goldberg, who translated Yiddish poet Avrom Sutzkever, as did Boris Pasternak; Saul Bellow, Cynthia Ozick, and Irving Howe translated from Yiddish; American poets Stanley Kunitz and Robert Pinsky, who rendered Anna Akhmatova and Dante from Russian and Italian, respectively; Nelly Sachs, who translated between Swedish and German; and Joseph Brodsky, who translated Juan Ramón Jiménez from Spanish into Russian.

Jewish languages, particularly Yiddish and modern Hebrew, have seen translation as a conduit for their cosmopolitanism. To think of Yiddish is to think of an unimpeded river of translation. Almost every significant literary work, from Baruch Spinoza's *Ethics* and Miguel de Cervantes's *Don Quixote* to Dostoyevsky's *Crime and Punishment,* Saint Exúpery's *The Little Prince,* and J. K. Rowling's *Harry Potter* saga, was rendered in Yiddish. A highlight in the tradition of Jewish translation is the Yiddish version of Shakespeare's *Hamlet,* done by I. J. Schwartz in 1918. The title page comes with a qualifier: "*fartaytsht un farbesert,*" translated and improved. Similarly, the writers of the Hebrew renaissance were intent on making Hebrew a modern language by allowing it to catch up to other world languages through translation. Bialik took it on himself to translate the European classics into Hebrew, including Heinrich Heine's poetry, Shakespeare's *Julius Caesar,* and Cervantes's *Don Quixote.* He believed the only way to advance a Hebrew language consciousness was by bringing Western civilization into it and allowing the biblical tongue to come to the present. He was a careful, lyrical translator. Along the same lines, Saul Tchernikhovsky translated the *Iliad* and the *Odyssey,* as well as Sophocles, Horace, Shakespeare, Molière, Pushkin, Goethe, Byron, Shelley, the Kalevala, the *Gilgamesh* cycle, and the Icelandic *Edda.* Likewise, Dvora Baron rendered Flaubert's *Madame Bovary* into Hebrew; and Leah Goldberg, who knew seven languages, translated Petrarch, Shakespeare, Tolstoy, Chekhov, Akhmatova, and Thomas Mann.

There is another facet in the history of Jewish literary translation: self-translation in particular, also called autotranslation. In the Jewish literary tradition, the number of writers who have switched languages and, along the way, translated their own oeuvre from one language to another, is large. Yiddish writers like Mendele Mokher Sforim and Sholem Aleichem themselves made Hebrew versions of novels originally written in Yiddish, and occasionally the other way around. Exiled by the Soviet Union, Joseph Brodsky wrote in English while he lived in America, but he never abandoned his native Russian, often retranslating an English-language poem back to Russian.

Self-translation has its drawbacks. In a typical translation, the translator brings to the text a new set of eyes. Translators look at the original as fixed, unalterable; their quest is to deliver the same content in the target language. But in autotranslations, the original is not necessarily fixed, since the author and translator are one and the same. It is therefore unsurprising that a self-translated book occasionally ends up reconfiguring the content of the original. See the references for a discussion of these and other related matters. Among the most controversial self-translators is Isaac Bashevis Singer. He started his career in Warsaw translating authors like Eric Maria Remarque from German into Yiddish. When he moved to America, at the age of thirty-five, at first he was shocked by the state of Yiddish in New York, which in his ears was a sign of pollution. He learned English but perhaps he had arrived too late to be fully fluent. Still, he understood that his best chance to make it as a contemporary writer was in English, Yiddish having been decimated by the Nazis during the Holocaust.

He devised a method he called "second originals." Almost all of his writing was published in the Yiddish newspaper *Forverts*, including his novels, which appeared in serialized form. Once they were out, Singer would collaborate with his English-language translators, often female and frequently possessing almost no knowledge of Yiddish, in bringing the work to an American audience. A typical session would be as follows: author and translator would meet at Singer's apartment in New York's Upper West Side; he would dictate, line by line, in imperfect English, the Yiddish original, while the translator transcribed the sentences; then the translator, at home, would type a clean version and bring it to Singer a short time later; the two would redraft that English version until Singer was satisfied. There are substantial discrepancies between the Yiddish and English versions of Singer's work, most of them entailing an overt desire to

Americanize—that is, to make palatable to English-language readers—the plot line. Singer, in the end, favored the latter, calling it his "second original." Most of the translators who rendered Singer's oeuvre into other languages, such as French, Italian, Spanish, Portuguese, and even his native Polish, were done, at his request, from the English versions.

Singer's New York in itself was vigorously multilingual. That, in part, is why Jews continue to feel the city's magnetism. In Jewish history, towns functioning like translation centers have existed since ancient times. The Talmudic academies of Sura and Pumbedita, in Babylon between 589 and 1038 CE, gathered an assortment of translators from different parts of the Middle East. During *La Convivencia*, the bastioned city of Toledo, in central Spain, was a hot spot where Hebrew, Arabic, Latin, and Spanish translators worked. Samuel ibn Tibbon, a twelfth-century translator who was based there and whose father was a distinguished translator, rendered into Hebrew, usually in a plain, unadorned, literal style, works such as Aristotle's *Meteorology* (1210), Maimonides's *Commentary on the Mishnah: Tractate Avot* (1202) and the *Guide for the Perplexed* (1204), and Islamic philosopher Averroes's *Abd Allah* (Three Treatises on Conjunction, ca. 1207), among others. New York assumed that mantle in the second half of the twentieth century, not necessarily because of the number of Jewish translators based there, but as a result of its location as America's publishing capital.

The translation of the Torah has always been at the heart of the Jewish translation tradition. As part of the Enlightenments, the French encyclopedists inspired versions into French, German, Italian, and other languages. And the Haskalah put to work Yiddish, Ladino, and other Jewish translators. Among the most famous translation of the Torah was the endeavor in 1925 of philosophers Martin Buber and Franz Rosenzweig, the latter the author of the treatise, *The Star of Redemption* (1919). Intriguingly, in their rendition they did not seek to bring biblical Hebrew into

9. A philosopher, compiler of Hasidic stories, and bible translator, Martin Buber, here browsing in a Jerusalem bookstore, believed in translation as an encounter between the reader and the divine.

present-day German. On the contrary, their innovative strategy, still employed in the early twenty-first century, was to recast the German language following the syntactical patterns of the Hebrew language, making German alien by means of Hebrew.

Buber's views on translation are linked to his thesis in his best-known work, *I and Thou* (1923), in which he explored how we engage with others—nature, people, the divine—as defining our sense of self. He explores three signifiers: "I," "Thou," and "It." Buber argued that these are not simply personal objects. We must learn to appreciate them as a "You." In his collaboration with Rosenzweig, Buber sought to distance the reader from the biblical text. He built a theological infrastructure to achieve this sense of alienation. Their translation achieves its objective by allowing the reader to come up with an individualized, unpredictable response to the original.

There have been numerous Jewish translators of the Hebrew Bible into English, in part or of the full text. The first was Isaac Leeser, who is regarded as a forerunner of modern Orthodox Judaism. Others include Aryeh Kaplan and Everett Fox. The most reliable—though, as in the other cases, not remotely as beautiful as the King James version—is *The Five Books of Moses* (2009) by Robert Alter. A Hebraist and literary critic with a fecund knowledge of the Jewish literary tradition—he wrote essays on Benjamin, Kafka, and Gershom Scholem, among others—Alter, in his version, is interested in philological meaning: What do words mean at various times? His commentary, at the bottom of the page, feels Talmudic though it concerns not only Jewish sources but also world culture in general.

Other momentous efforts are the translation of the Talmud. Making such nonlinear legalistic texts available to non-Hebrew and non-Aramaic reading audiences opens up new horizons to it. The twenty-two volumes appeared between 1989 and 2012, in English, French, Russian, and Spanish, with commentary by Adin Steinsaltz, a Jerusalem-based Chabad rabbi who studied mathematics, physics, and chemistry at Hebrew University. Likewise, the translation, in twelve volumes, of *Sefer ha-Zohar* (2003–18), the Kabbalistic source, by Daniel Matt, remains a landmark. Translation is never an innocent enterprise, though. In the Jewish literary tradition, a number of apparently straightforward translations have become controversial, a couple of which have been discussed earlier. These controversies showcase the degree to which the art of translation is, at its core, an effort to accommodate the message in the original to a different reader. That difference is not about subjectivity: readers are different from one another. I am referring to the way a work of literature might be reappraised in diverse milieus.

If a classic might be described as a book that survives in a plurality of languages thanks to translators, Sholem Aleichem's novel, a perennial favorite in the Jewish literary tradition, is a prime example. Originally written in Yiddish, *Tevye the Dairyman* has appeared in more than three dozen languages worldwide. In several of them, including English, there are numerous versions. Various incomplete early versions of Sholem Aleichem appeared in newspapers. A slew of translators followed: Frances Butwin (1949), Hillel Halkin (1987), Miriam Katz (1994), and Aliza Shevrin (2009). Each offers a different interpretation of Sholem Aleichem's masterpiece. That is, each is a reader unto their own. Although one might argue in favor of one or the other, what matters in the end is the plurality of possibilities. Other forms of translation catapulted *Tevye the Dairyman* into global recognition. The novel was adapted to the screen. In total, there are four versions: Yiddish (1939), Hebrew (1968), English (1971), and Russian (2017). Of course, the most popular adaptation is to theater, again in various formats, including *Fiddler on the Roof*, among the most beloved Broadway musicals ever. It has been staged all over the globe, including in Tokyo, New Delhi, and Mexico City. Translation, therefore, is nothing but tight, fateful, and meticulous reading. It is also an intervention on a text, a reimagining of it.

A similar discussion is appropriate in regard to Kafka's *The Metamorphosis*. It opens with one of the most famous lines in world literature, one that has given way to a plethora of interpretations: "Als Gregor Samsa eines Morgens aus unruhigen Träumen erwachte, fand er sich in seinem Bett zu einem ungeheueren Ungeziefer verwandelt." In German, the phrase *ungeheuren ungeziefer* means "large bug." It has been translated, among other ways, as bug, cockroach, and vermin. The semantic ambivalence is important in that it visualizes Samsa, who is never defined in Jewish terms, as amorphous, in itself a statement about Jewish identity. Edwin and Willa Muir's 1933 version opened the gates in English: "As Gregor Samsa awoke one morning from uneasy dreams he found himself transformed in his bed into a giant insect." Among other translators, this was followed by Stanley Corngold (1972): "When Gregor Samsa woke up one morning from unsettling dreams, he found himself changed in his bed into a monstrous vermin"; Joaquim Neugroschel (1993): "One morning, upon awakening from agitated dreams, Gregor Samsa found himself, in his bed, transformed into a monstrous vermin"; Michael Hoffman (2007): "When Gregor Samsa awoke one morning from troubled dreams, he found himself changed into a monstrous cockroach in his bed"; Joyce Crick (2009): "As Gregor Samsa woke one morning from uneasy dreams, he found himself transformed into some kind of monstrous vermin"; Christopher Moncrieff (2014): "One morning, as Gregor Samsa woke from a fitful, dream-filled sleep, he found that he had changed into an enormous bedbug"; Susan Bernofsky (also 2014): "When Gregor Samsa woke one morning from troubled dreams, he found himself transformed right there in his bed into some sort of monstrous insect"; and John R. Williams (once more 2014): "One morning Gregor Samsa woke in his bed from uneasy dreams and found he had turned into a large verminous insect."

Insect, vermin, cockroach—the differences in Samsa's portrait between all these approaches is not subtle. The plurality of interpretations point to the Talmudic nature of the endeavor. In and of itself, translation is neither an act nor an art that is specifically Jewish. Yet at its core it defines that diasporic experience, highlighting not only the multilingual quality of aterritorial life but also the layers of meaning every language accumulates over time. Chaim Nakhman Bialik once said that whoever approaches Judaism through translation is kissing a woman through a veil. In Israel, the claim is frequently adapted to poetry: translating it means recognizing that an aspect of it will forever be concealed. In *Don Quixote*, Cervantes offers a similar image. He suggests that reading a work in translation is the equivalent of looking at a Flemish tapestry from the back. The effort, needless to say, is better than nothing.

There is another facet worth noting about the translation life: translingualism. It is not particular to Jewish literature but it features prominently in it. Some writers deliver their work in more than one language, say Hebrew and Yiddish (Sholem Aleichem), or Ladino and German (Canetti), or Russian and English (Brodsky), or Spanish and English (Dorfman). Others switch from their mother tongue to another language as a result of immigration or for personal reasons or because they are eager to reach a different, perhaps wider, audience. Or they are citizens in countries with multiple languages, one of them used by the majority and others embraced by minorities. Indeed, the minority-versus-minority dichotomy is a feature of Jewish identity: Kafka was from Prague, yet wrote not in Czech but in German. These negotiations prove that translation is not a profession, but a way of being.

Along the way, it is worth pondering: Might a translation be better than the original? Furthermore, could it even usurp the place of the original? In the vicissitudes of Jewish literature, ancient and modern, this is rather common. The English version of the Talmud is infinitely more readable than the Aramaic in which it was delivered. In the twentieth century, renditions of Singer's stories were, frankly, often better than his Yiddish versions, the prime example being Bellow's "Gimpel the Fool." The same goes for other writers. Of course, the reverse is true too: given his biblical resonances, translating Agnon out of Hebrew is always a form of diminishment; likewise, Canetti loses gravitas when deprived of his German voice. In any case, the translator, regardless of the outcome, is as personal as anyone gets with a text.

Chapter 10
The letterless canon

In the twenty-first century, it is clear Jews are not only the People of the Book. The concept of book—the technological device through which knowledge is traditionally disseminated—has evolved. Audiences have changed. A book now might be a comic strip, a graphic novel, or audible. It might show up on paper, on screen, or on a tablet. It might use images or video or be electronic. The Jewish children's book industry exploded in the previous century. Its audience might be children.

Let's start with children's books. While children are at the center of several Jewish holidays, including Passover, Purim, Tuvishvat, and Hanukah, for millennia, children-oriented books were limited to the Passover *Haggadah*, which retells the odyssey of the Israelites as slaves in Egypt and the drive by their political leader Moses from bondage into freedom through a tortuous passage across the Red Sea and into the desert. From the Middle Ages onward, the Passover story was told by means of alternating illuminated scenes with prayers, midrash, and other commentary. In a rudimentary way, such juxtaposition was an incipient version of what came to be known as the picture book, a narrative targeted to young readers, from two years old to the teens. And among Yiddish speakers, the *Alef-Beis*, an easy-to-handle literacy booklet, was another type of children's book. The arrival of children's books is the result of dramatic cultural changes, including Sigmund Freud's psychoanalytic theories of childhood, advancement in education, and civil rights efforts to stop child labor during the Industrial Revolution. It has much to do with accelerated technological advances in printing color books at affordable prices. In Poland, Russia, France, Germany, and other countries, Jewish authors and illustrators—Marc Chagall among them—were at the forefront of this new type of literature.

Among the most successful Jewish picture books, one with a decidedly Jewish theme that manifests itself symbolically, is *Curious George* (1939–69), written and illustrated by Margret Rey and H. A. Rey. The character, a rascal of a monkey, uses a bicycle and other means of transport to ingeniously escape compromising situations. The story of how the character, George (the character was first called "Fifi" in French and, later, "Zozo" in English), who is said to have been found in Africa by a man with a yellow hat, who transports him to a big city to live in a zoo, came to be is in itself curious. Margret Elisabeth Waldstein and Hans Augusto Reyersbach met in Hamburg, Germany. They published their first story, "Cecily G. and the Nine Monkeys," in French while living in Paris. With the imminent arrival of the Nazis, they were forced to leave on makeshift bicycles with the manuscript of *Curious George*. They made their way to Brazil, where they reunited, and from there traveled to the United States, settling in Cambridge, Massachusetts. Their own ordeal as Jews, finding how to run away from threat through adventurous strategies, is thus ingrained in their character's traits. That survival strategy mirrors the path of Jews in modern history, from one challenge to another. *Curious George*, which, aside from books, has been adapted into movies, television shows, and museum exhibits, is now a worldwide franchise that displays the way Jewish literature for children incarnates countless platforms.

Among the most untraditional of Jewish children's books is *Where the Wild Things Are* (1963). Inspired by Holocaust survivors, Maurice Sendak built it as a *bildungsroman* that centers on a little boy, Max, who, throwing a tantrum as his mother calls him for dinner, ends up in his room alone, where he promises not to cooperate with his mother. The dialogue between text and pictures allows Sendak to break molds. Images threaten to reach beyond the edges of the book itself, just as Max is looking to explore the limits of his universe. Max's room is his domain. As the narrative progresses, the room mutates into a forest, complete with a boat. Max sails to a faraway land where he meets endearing wild creatures, monsters (in Yiddish, *vilde khayes*) whom he befriends and soon becomes the leader of. But after a while Max feels lonely. He wants to see his mother again. He wants the comfort of his home, in particular his room. And so, he ventures back with the support of the wild things, until he rejoins his mother for dinner. A story of rebellion, Sendak's book is an adventure in which the protagonist finds his own limits as an individual. It is about the world as a strange, complex, menacing universe and about home as a secure place. In countless ways, *Where the Wild Things Are* is a Jewish story: Max is an individual who needs to test himself in a foreign milieu; he feels the need to find his true worth; only then will he be able to find solace in his own sense of self.

Another prime example of allegory for Jewish children, *The Phantom Tollbooth* (1961), by Norton Juster, focuses on word play and indulges in the precise, mathematical humor of Lewis Carroll (Juster was an architect). It tells the story of Milo, a San Francisco boy, who after receiving a mysterious package goes into a wild, unexpected odyssey. His itinerary resembles the twists and turns of diaspora life. One characteristic of Jewish children's books is the astounding diversity in content. Stories might deal with the Old Country, baseball, friendship, race, sexuality, anti-Semitism, and the countless challenges of growing up. Judy Blume discussed topics as diverse as menstruation, birth control, death, and faith in God in her children's and young adult books. Stan and Jan Berenstain created a series called *The Berenstain Bears*. Their ordeals allowed young readers to deal with fear, change, and hope.

Black Jewish writers like Julius Lester, who, during the civil rights era, converted to Judaism and often reflected on the plight of Israelites as indentured labor in Egypt, in *To Be a Slave* (1968) employed the format of children's storytelling to enter the perspective of a slave during colonial times.

An outgrowth of Jewish literature are superheroes; this might seem surprising, yet it is a logical response to adversity. Superman is a perfect example. His creators were Joe Shuster, a Toronto-born Jew, the child of Dutch and Ukrainian immigrants, and his friend Jerry Siegel, the Cleveland-born child of Lithuanian immigrants. They met in their teens, joined by a shared passion for science fiction and the movies. Adept at drawing, the sold their art to various companies, including DC Comics, at a time when comics were taking off as an industry. The first episode of *Superman* came out in 1938. It is not difficult to see the qualities that characterize Superman as directly linked to Jewish vulnerability in the middle of the twentieth century. Hitler was already in power then. Unlike the typical nerdy Jewish character, physically clumsy, facing adversity by activating the mind, Superman is superhuman. A descendent of the golem, he has a double identity and is chosen to perform his good deeds out of that duality. He is, after all, an immigrant from another planet, Krypton. In turn, authors like Michael Chabon have innovated by turning their fascination with the world of Jewish comic-strip artists into novelistic explorations. *The Amazing Adventures of Kavalier and Clay* (2000) focuses on two cousins, Joe Kavalier and Sammy Clay, the first Czech, the second from Brooklyn, whose art is part of the book of comics in the so-called golden age, around the time of the Second World War.

A logical outgrowth of comic strips are graphic novels. The father of the genre is Will Eisner, who, having started his career in comics, moved into book-length explorations of Jewish life using illustrations. Deeply existential, his books *A Contract with God* (1978), which includes four stand-alone stories, among them the eponymous tale about a religious man who gives up his faith after the death of his young adopted daughter; and *Fagin the Jew* (2003), in which Eisner retells the story of Charles Dickens's anti-Semitic character Fagin in *Oliver Twist* (1838), invoke, overtly and otherwise, the nuanced life in the New York tenements depicted, among others, in Henry Roth's novel *Call It Sleep*. Eisner, who to such degree became synonymous with the comic book that a national prize to the creative achievement in that realm carries his name, also published a study of anti-Semitism called *The Plot: The Secret Story of the Protocols of the Elders of Zion* (2005).

With a style capable of supreme plasticity, Eisner opened the door for historical explorations using images and words, as is the case of Art Spiegelman's *Maus*, Alison Bechdel's *Fun Home: A Family Tragicomic* (2006), as well as *El Iluminado*, about Luis de Carvajal the Younger. All of this makes literature, as an artistic manifestation, more elastic. Along these lines, the contributions to popular culture made by Jews to American comics—particularly to the superhero genre—must be emphasized. One example among many is *Stan Lee*, whose Jewish creations (*Spider-Man*, *X-Men*, *The Hulk*, and *Fantastic Four*) revised biblical and rabbinic stories. Likewise, *Mad Magazine*, helped to loosen up some of the 1950s-era conformism.

One should go further. Is comedy, for instance, an extension of this tradition? My answer is yes. Stand-up comedy, a popular narrative form, became a fertile turf for Jews in the mid-twentieth century. One of the most magnetic milieus for Jewish comedy was the so-called Borscht Belt in the Catskill Mountains region of Upstate New York. It is there where stand-up comedians, the majority of them male, like the Marx Brothers, Jack Benny, George Burns, Milton Berle, Sid Caesar, Lenny Bruce, Jerry Lewis, Mel Brooks, and Woody Allen, in front of live audiences, would freely associate about entering the American midstream with a slapstick approach, in a hodgepodge of sexual, domestic, financial,

10. A page from *A Contract with God*, by Will Eisner, in which an
elderly Jewish immigrant in the New York tenement, like Job in the
Bible, laments his fate to the almighty. Eisner, considered the father
of the contemporary graphic novel, published such narratives as
A Contract with God and *The Plot: The Secret History of the Protocols of
the Elders of Zion* to encourage a deeper, widespread engagement with
Jewish civilization.

political, religious, and linguistic material. Quickly, that kind of humor transcended the region—the audience was mostly composed of New York Jews on summer vacation—to become a staple of radio, television, and the movies. The Borscht Belt opened the door and defined the role and style of subsequent Jewish comedians. They include Larry David, Jerry Seinfeld, and Sarah Silverman. They all transitioned into successful television personalities with shows like *Seinfeld* (1989–98), *Curb Your Enthusiasm* (2000–2011), and *The Sarah Silverman Program* (2007–10). They all take the anarchism inherited from the previous generation of Jewish humorists to the next level. Emblematically, Seinfeld's show is built around the concept of four close adult friends living in Manhattan. The premise is that "nothing happens" in the episodes, nothing, that is, other than the friends sharing with one another their daily annoyances. It might be shown, judging from narrative artifacts such as these, the degree to which Jews made it to the nation's mainstream: their distinct sensibility broke cultural borders, embraced by everyone, regardless of religion.

Several of these Jewish comedians went on to become national icons. Lewis made dozens of comedies about forgetful professors and other stereotypical characters. Brooks made movies with a distinctively Jewish sensibility, like *The Producers* (1967), about a Jewish Broadway impresario intent on creating a musical flop that ends up being about Adolf Hitler. Allen turned himself into a stunningly prolific film director whose numerous movies, from *All You Ever Wanted to Know about Sex* (1972) to *Hannah and Her Sisters* (1986), assess the layers of modern anxiety, frequently through a schlemiel-like character, played by Allen himself, whose intellectual and erotic adventures end in frustration. The storytelling quality of Brooks's play springs for the use of Jewish humor, in life as in literature, as a response to catastrophe.

This places Jewish literature in the realm of Hollywood. The production studios, formed in the early twentieth century, had important Jewish producers as key players. The same is to be said about film directors, in America and beyond, as diverse as Ernst Lubitsch, Josef von Sternberg, George Cukor, Billy Wilder, Stanley Kubrick, Steven Spielberg, and Joel and Ethan Coen, or the hundreds of Jewish screenwriters. As in books, Jewish filmmaking is a narrative quest that is less about content than it is about sensibility. Combining traits from television and film, in their relatively brief life, streaming services—Netflix, HBO, Hulu, and others—have exploded as a global form of entertainment as well as intellectual and artistic exploration that, when addressing Jewish and Israeli topics, borrows from literary sources. Ori Elon and Yehonatan Indursky's *Shtisel* (2013–16) looks at rebellion in an ultra-Orthodox environment. Jill Soloway's *Transparent* (2014–19) explores intricate sexual preferences in an American Jewish family that are becoming increasingly more standard. Lior Raz and Avi Issacharoff's *Fauda* (2015–) delves into the Israel Defense Forces. And Anna Winger's *Unorthodox* (2020) looks at the life of an orthodox female renegade traveling from New York to Germany.

If, indeed, these are variations of literary artifacts, Jewish literature requires a broader, all-encompassing definition, one that keeps up with evolving views of an audience's consumption. The basic tenet, however, remains the same: In what way does a story convey values that travel through time yet are in constant renewal?

Epilogue: On to the future

In 1946, French existential philosopher Jean-Paul Sartre released a short book called *Réflexions sur la question juive*, known in English as *Anti-Semite and Jew*. It was the year after the Second World War. Facetiously, Sartre argued that Jews and anti-Semites live in a symbiotic relationship: to exist, one needs the other. While easy to debunk (for starters, there have never been Jews who have no antagonists), such a theory is a useful tool to explore the labyrinthine paths of Jewish literature. Looking at it in toto, one does find, it is true, an embedded mechanism whereby Jewish characters, from Sholem Aleichem's Tevye to Saul Bellow's Herzog, are in constant conversation, real or imagined, with their own absence, the idea that their diasporic life might suddenly come to an end. There are also dialogues with concrete aggressors.

Since the beginning, Jews have made up a minuscule portion of humankind: at any given time, the total is less than 0.01 percent. Since Babylonian times, war, natural disasters, and assimilation, voluntary or though forced conversion, have forced the Jewish minority to survive. While disaster lurks nearby, life continues. It is precisely that fragility, the sense that tomorrow is not assured, that keeps Jews always on the edge. For literature, that duality, that precariousness, is invaluable. It is a kind of internal clock driven by performance: Jews live in order to make themselves noticed, to themselves and others, and they make themselves noticed in order to live. For writers, that performance is composed of words. As Grace Paley puts it in the epigraph to this volume, which is part of the interview series "The Art of Fiction" in *The Paris Review* (Fall 1992), "Write what will stop your breath if you don't write." She adds, "Art is too long and life is too short."

For the members of *Am Ha-Sefer*, the prophets of doom are perennially around the corner. Those prophets might themselves be Jews. In his introduction to his anthology *Jewish-American Stories* (1977), Irving Howe stated that "Jewish American fiction has moved beyond its high point." About fifteen years later, another American Jewish critic, Leslie Fiedler, made a similar statement: "The Jewish American novel is over and done with, a part of history rather than a living literature." These kinds of statements, not only about Jewish writing in the United States but also about the rest of the world, are dead wrong. The reasons are simple: the DNA of Jews is marked by perseverance; and even in the most adventitious of circumstances, Jewish literature is a chronicle of survival. The eternal questions—Am I a Jew? What is home?—are not going away.

It is now fitting to return to the three questions posed at the outset: What makes modern Jewish literature modern? In what way is it Jewish? And how to understand literature at a time like ours in which the traditional book is constantly being redefined? The task of writing a Very Short Introduction for a topic as broad and deep as modern Jewish literature seems impossible. In regard to modernity, my approach has been to begin from 1492, which, granted, is atypical. The majority of historians prefer to start on or shortly before the French Revolution. I provide a rationale for this approach that, I hope, is both concise and convincing, certainly in terms of the volume's organization. Conceptually, the questions of how to define literature in general and what makes a Jewish literary work Jewish are at the core of Jewish civilization. After all, this is a chance to synthesize what often appears muddy to the general eye. Even though I have mostly focused on traditional literary forms, I have invited readers to think of literature in the twenty-first century as far more: graphic novels, film scripts, stand-up comedy and different types of performance, and even tweets and other forms of social media. I have also suggested that nonfiction works by Spinoza, Mendelssohn, Freud, Marx, Arendt, Benjamin, and other philosophers and critics are an integral part of this tradition, as are feminists like Gloria Steinem and Betty Friedan. In what might be called the anthological imagination, I have proposed the work of Agnon, Bialik, Howe, and other editors of literary omnibuses as equally worthy creators. I have made references to radio and television, which I also consider literary artifacts. If this ever-expanding view of literature generates discomfort among traditionalists, so be it.

As for what makes a particular work Jewish, among the accepted definition is Dan Miron's suggestion that a literary work is Jewish if it "evinces an interest in or is in whatever way and to whatever extent conditioned by a sense of *Judesein*, being Jewish, or is being read by readers who experience it as if it showed interest and were conditioned by the writer's being Jewish." This is not a perfect definition—there is a lot of vagueness here—yet the notion of *Judesein* seems valuable in that it allows for not only critics but also readers in general to determine the reception of what "being Jewish" means. I believe it is important to be more precise. As I have shown in examples from Franz Kafka, Isaac Babel, and Bruno Schulz to Elias Canetti, Susan Sontag, and Woody Allen, a Jewish work of literature, in my view, is defined as such by a combination of content, authorship, and readership. In their degrees of assimilation, Jews oscillate between outspoken loyalty to the tribe and outright rejection or ignorance even outright ignorance of one's origins. Still, the Jewish sensibility has a way of filtering itself, at least in the perspective of those receiving a work of literature.

Like the Talmud before it, Jewish literature, since 1492, and particularly as a result of the Haskalah, is made of a symphony of voices, each located in different times and places. Haphazardly, these voices interact with each other in dozens of languages, meeting in the reader's mind through translation. As they learn, borrow, or steal from one another, they chronicle life in all its minutia. Jewish literature, in short, is Jewish memory. This is what the protagonist of Isaac Babel's "Story of My Dovecot" understands as "the obligation to remember everything." And this is what historian Hayim Yosef Yerushalmi refers to in his book *Zakhor* as the art of turning the world into word. A colossal demographic realignment of the Jewish map took place between 1885 and 1945. Who would have imagined that by the end of that period about half of the Ashkenazi population in Eastern Europe and its Sephardic counterpart in the orbits of the Ottoman Empire would be annihilated, that the other half would migrate to establish new centers in the Americas, Africa, Australia, and elsewhere, and that Israel, a free, autonomous Jewish nation, would flourish—not without contestation—in the biblical land? Well, a few did imagine it. For instance, A. Ansky, in *Khurbn Galicia*, sought to create an ethnographic tapestry of the poor, pogrom-ridden Jewish villages in Galicia-Volhynia in the border today between Poland and Ukraine, fearing it was too fragile to last long. All this is to say that Jewish life, as we know it now, is as fleeting as in any previous period in history. About three of every ten Jews live in Israel in the first quarter of the twenty-first century. For the rest, aterritoriality—which pivots back to Borges's lecture "The Argentine Writer and Tradition," in which he includes a quote by sociologist Thorstein Veblen arguing that what distinguishes Jews in Western culture is that "they act in that culture and at the same time do not feel tied to it"—is still the sine qua non of Jewish life, as it has been for millennia.

Even modern Hebrew literature engages deeply with the diasporic quality of Jewish life. As Israel insists on breaking with the idea of homelessness as a consistent theme throughout the history of Jewish literature, it de facto becomes an iteration of the same motif. Or else, it might be argued that Israeli literature, despite or perhaps because of its biblical roots, is not even "Jewish" anymore, since it holds to a specific, particular territoriality. But that seems nearsighted, since modern Hebrew writers are constantly seeing themselves in dialogue with world literature in general and with diaspora Jewish literature in particular.

In any case, aterritoriality means that in the blink of an eye, diaspora life will yet again be in need of reinvention. Years from now, the current centers of Jewish life like New York, Buenos Aires, and Tel-Aviv will become foregone chapters in the history of Jewish literature, the way Toledo, Warsaw, and Berlin were in the past. Judging from precedent, storytelling is likely to be rekindled elsewhere to keeps Jews alive.

References

Introduction

Jorge Luis Borges, "The Argentine Writer and Tradition," in *Labyrinths: Selected Stories & Other Writings*, ed. Donald A. Yates and James E. Irby (New York: New Directions, 1964), 62.

George Steiner, *Extraterritorial: Papers on Literature and the Language Revolution* (New York: Athenaeum, 1971), 27.

Chapter 1

Yehuda Halevi, "My Heart Is in the East," in *Selected Translations: Poems, 2000–2020*, trans. Ilan Stavans (Pittsburgh, PA: University of Pittsburgh Press, 2021), 46.

Ilan Stavans, *Quixote: The Novel and the World* (New York: W. W. Norton, 2015).

Chapter 3

Albert Einstein, *Ideas and Opinions* (New York: Crown, 1995), 45.

Letter from Hannah Arendt to Salman Schocken, August 9, 1946. Schocken Book Archive, New York. In Franz Kafka, *The Castle*, trans. Mark Harman (New York: Schocken Books, 1998), vii–ix.

Franz Kafka, *Complete Stories*, ed. Nahum H. Glazer (New York: Schocken Books, 1963), 245–46.

Chapter 4

Hannah Arendt, *Eichman in Jerusalem*, 2nd ed. (New York: Schocken Books, 1968), 78.

Marie Luise Knott, ed., *Hannah Arendt and Gerschom Scholem: Correspondence*, trans. Anthony David (Chicago: University of Chicago Press, 2017).

Chapter 5

Emma Lazarus, "The New Colossus" and "1492," in *Selected Poems*, ed. Esther Shor (New York: Library of America, 2005), 67, 72.

Saul Bellow, ed., *Great Jewish Short Stories* (New York: Dell, 1963), xii.

Saul Bellow, *The Adventures of Augie March* (New York: Viking, 1953), 3.

Chapter 6

Saul Bellow, *To Jerusalem and Back: A Personal Account* (New York: Viking, 1976).

John Felstiner, "Writing Zion: An Exchange between Paul Celan and Yehuda Amichai," *The New Republic*, June 5, 2006, https://newrepublic.com/article/65477/writing-zion.

Chapter 7

Ilan Stavans, *The Seventh Heaven: Travels through Jewish Latin America* (Pittsburgh, PA: University of Pittsburgh Press, 2019).

Chapter 8

Susan Sontag, *Regarding the Pain of Others* (New York: Farrar, Straus and Giroux, 2003), 39.

Chapter 9

Robert Carroll and Stephen Prickett, eds., *The Bible: Authorized King James Version* (Oxford: Oxford University Press, 2008), 3.

George Steiner, *After Babel: Aspects of Language and Translation* (Oxford: Oxford University Press, 1975), 15.

Jacques Derrida, *Monolingualism of the Other*, trans. Patrick Mensah (Stanford, CA: Stanford University Press, 1998), 7.

Ludwig Wittgenstein, *Tractatus Logico-Philosophicus*, trans. D. F. Pears and B. F. McGuinness, intro. Bertrand Russell (London: Routledge, 2014), 7.

Emmanuel Levinas, *The Levinas Reader*, ed. Seán Hand (Hoboken, NJ: Blackwell, 1989), 98.

Jacques Derrida, *Of Grammatology*, trans. Gayatri Chakravorty Spivak, intro. Judith Butler (Baltimore: Johns Hopkins University Press, 2016), 32.

Ilan Stavans, *On Self-Translation: Meditations on Language* (Albany: State University of New York Press, 2018).

Ilan Stavans, "Translating Tevye," in *Singer's Typewriter and Mine: Reflections on Jewish Culture* (Lincoln: University of Nebraska Press, 2012), 82–87.

Franz Kafka, *Die Verwandlung* (Munich Kurt Wolff, 1915); *The Metamorphosis*, trans. Edwin Muir and Willa Muir (New York: Shocken Books, 1933); trans. Stanley Corngold (New York: Modern Library, 1972); trans. Joachim Neugroschel (New York: Scribner, 1993); trans. Michael Hofmann (New York: Penguin Modern Classics, 2007); trans. Joyce Crick (Oxford: Oxford World Classics, 2009); trans. Christopher Moncrieff (London: Alma Classics, 2014); trans. Susan Bernofsky (New York: W. W. Norton, 2014); and trans. John R. Williams (Knoxville, TN: Wordsworth Classic, 2014).

Epilogue

Jonathan Dee, Barbara Jones, and Larissa MacFarquhar, "The Art of Fiction: Grace Paley," *The Paris Review*, no. 124 (Fall 1992): 136.

Irving Howe, "Introduction," *Jewish American Stories* (New York: Signet, 1977), xix.

Leslie Fieldler, *Fiedler on the Roof: Essays on Literature and Jewish Identity* (Boston: David R. Godine, 1991), 76.

Dan Miron, *From Continuity to Contiguity: Toward a New Jewish Literary Thinking* (Stanford, CA: Stanford University Press, 2010), 405.

Isaac Babel, "Story of My Dovecot," in *Collected Works*, ed. Natalie Babel, trans. Peter Constantine (New York: W. W. Norton, 2002), 198.

Further reading

Given the expansive span of modern Jewish literature, this is an abbreviated bibliography that highlights a few of the essential voices. The inclusion of anthologies in the section "Primary Sources" is meant to serve as a menu of possibilities.

Primary Sources

Agnon, Shmuel Yosef. *A Bridal Canopy*. Translated by I. M. Lask. Garden City, NY: Doubleday, Doran, 1937.

Agnon, Shmuel Yosef, ed. *Days of Awe; Being a Treasury of Traditions, Legends and Learned Commentaries Concerning Roth ha-Shanah, Yom Kippur and the Days in between, Culled from Three Hundred Volumes, Ancient and New*. New York: Schocken Books, 1948.

Aleichem, Sholem. *Tevye the Dairyman and Motl the Cantor's Son*. Translated by Aliza Shevrin. Introduction by Dan Miron. New York: Penguin Classics, 2009.

Alter, Robert, trans. and com. *The Five Books of Moses: A Translation with Commentary*. New York: W. W. Norton, 2004.

Anonymous. *Lazarillo de Tormes*. Edited and translated by Ilan Stavans. New York: Norton Critical Editions, 2016.

Arendt, Hannah. *Eichmann in Jerusalem: A Report on the Banality of Evil*. New York: Viking, 1963.

Babel, Isaac. *Collected Works*. Edited by Natalie Babel. Translated by Peter Constantine. Introduction by Cynthia Ozick. New York: W. W. Norton, 2002.

Bassani, Giorgio. *The Garden of the Finzi-Continis*. Translated by William Weaver. New York: Harcourt Brace Jovanovich, 1977.

Bechdel, Alison. *Fun Home: A Family Tragicomic.* Boston: Houghton Mifflin, 2006.

Bellow, Saul. *The Adventures of Augie March.* New York: Viking, 1953.

Bellow, Saul, ed. *Great Jewish Short Stories.* New York: Dell, 1963.

Bellow, Saul. *Herzog.* New York: Viking, 1964.

Bellow, Saul. *To Jerusalem and Back: A Personal Account.* New York: Viking, 1976.

Benjamin, Walter. *Illuminations.* Edited and with an introduction by Hannah Arendt. Translated by Harry Zohn. New York: Schocken Books, 1968.

Benjamin, Walter. *Reflections.* Edited and with an introduction by Peter Demetz. Translated by Edmund Jephcott. New York: Harcourt Brace Jovanovich, 1978.

Bialik, Chaim Nakhman. *Selected Poems.* Edited and translated by Atar Hadari. Introduction by Dan Miron. Syracuse, NY: Syracuse University Press, 2000.

Bialik, Chaim Nachman, with Eliezer Ravnitzky, eds. *The Book of Legends.* New York: Schocken Books, 1992.

Buber, Martin. *I and Thou.* Translated by Walter Kaufmann. New York: Scribner, 1970.

Buber, Martin, ed. *Tales of the Hasidim.* Foreword by Chaim Potok. New York: Schocken Books, 1991.

Canetti, Elias. *Auto-da-fé.* Translated by C. V. Wedgwood. New York: Farrar, Straus, and Giroux, 1984.

Canetti, Elias. *The Memoirs of Elias Canetti: The Tongue Set Free, The Torch in My Ear, The Play of the Eyes.* Translated by Joachim Neugroschel. New York: Farrar, Straus, and Giroux, 1999.

Carmi, T., ed. *The Penguin Book of Hebrew Poetry.* New York: Viking, 1981.

Cole, Peter, trans. *The Dream of the Poem: Hebrew Poetry from Muslin and Christian Spain, 950–1492.* Princeton, NJ: Princeton University Press, 2007.

Derrida, Jacques. *Monolingualism of the Other.* Translated by Patrick Mensah. Stanford, CA: Stanford University Press, 1998.

Derrida, Jacques. *Of Grammatology.* Translated by Gayatri Chakravorty Spivak. Introduction by Judith Butler. Baltimore: Johns Hopkins University Press, 2016.

Einstein, Albert. *Ideas and Opinions.* New York: Crown, 1995.

Eisner, Will. *A Contract with God and Other Tenement Stories.* New York: W. W. Norton, 2017.

Eisner, Will. *Fagin the Jew.* New York: Doubleday, 2003.

Felstiner, John. *Paul Celan: Poet, Survivor, Jew*. New Haven, CT: Yale University Press, 1995.

Frank, Ana. *Diary of a Young Girl: Definitive Edition*. Edited by Otto H. Frank and Miriam Pressler. Translated by Susan Massotty. New York: Bantam, 1997.

Freud, Sigmund. *Basic Writings*. Translated by A. A. Brill. New York: Modern Library, 1995.

Friedan, Betty. *The Feminine Mystique*. New York: W. W. Norton, 1963.

Ginzburg, Natalia. *Family Lexicon*. Translated by Jenny McPhee. New York: New York Review of Books, 2017.

Glikl of Hamel. *Memoirs, 1691–1719*. Annotated and with an introduction by Chava Turniansky. Translated by Sara Friedman. Waltham, MA: Brandeis University Press, 2019.

Grossman, David. *Falling Out of Time*. Translated by Jessica Cohen. New York: Alfred A. Knopf, 2014. Reprint, Waltham, MA: Brandeis University Press, 2019.

Grossman, David. *See Under: Love*. Translated by Betsy Rosenberg. New York: Farrar, Straus and Giroux, 1989.

Herzl, Theodor. *Altneuland*. Translated by Paula Arnold. Haifa, Israel: Haifa Publications, 1960.

Herzl, Theodor. *The Jews' State*. Translated with an introduction by Henk Overberg. Northvale, NJ: Jason Aronson, 1997.

Howe, Irving, ed. *Jewish American Stories*. New York: Signet, 1977.

Howe, Irving. *World of Our Fathers: The Journey of East European Jews to America and the Life They Found and Made*. New York: Harcourt Brace Jovanovich, 1976.

Howe, Irving, with Eliezer Greenberg, eds. *A Treasury of Yiddish Stories*. New York: Meridian Books, 1958.

Howe, Irving, with Ruth R. Wisse and Khrone Shmeruk, eds. *The Penguin Book of Modern Yiddish Verse*. New York: Viking, 1987.

Jabotinsky, Vladimir. *The Jewish War Front*. London: Allen & Unwin, 1940.

Jacobson, Howard. *The Finkler Question*. London: Bloomsbury, 2010.

Jacobson, Roman. *Selected Writings*. Edited by Stephen Rudy. 6 vols. The Hague: Mouton, 1971–85.

Kafka, Franz. *America: The Man Who Disappeared*. Translated with an introduction by Michael Hofmann. New York: New Directions, 2002.

Kafka, Franz. *The Castle*. Translation by Mark Harman. New York: Schocken Books, 1998.

Kafka, Franz. *Complete Stories*. Edited by Nahum H. Glazer. Introduction by John Updike. New York: Schocken Books, 1983.

Kafka, Franz. *The Metamorphosis*. Translated by Susan Bernofsky. New York: W. W. Norton, 2014.

Kafka, Franz. *The Trial*. Translated by Breon Mitchell. New York: Schocken Books, 1998.

Klein, A. M. *The Second Scroll*. Marlboro, VT: Marlboro Press, 1985.

Lazarus, Emma. *Selected Poems*. Edited by Esther Schor. New York: Library of America, 2005.

Leftwich, Joseph. *Yisröel: The First Jewish Omnibus*. London: J. Heritage, 1933.

Levi, Primo. *Collected Works*. 3 vols. Translated by Ann Goldstein. Introduction by Toni Morrison. New York: W. W. Norton, 2015.

Levinas, Emmanuel. *The Levinas Reader*. Edited by Seán Hand. Oxford: Blackwell, 1989.

Malamud, Bernard. *Collected Stories*. Edited by Robert Giroux. New York: Farrar, Straus and Giroux, 1997.

Modiano, Patrick. *In the Café of Lost Youth*. Translated by Chris Clarke. New York: New York Review Books, 2016.

Modiano, Patrick. *The Search Warrant*. Translated by Joanna Kilmartin. New York: Random House, 2000.

Oz, Amos. *The Amos Oz Reader*. Edited by Nitza Ben-Tov. Boston: Houghton Mifflin Harcourt, 2009.

Ozick, Cynthia. *A Cynthia Ozick Reader*. Edited by Elaine M. Kauvar. Bloomington: Indiana University Press, 1996.

Ozick, Cynthia. *The Shawl*. New York: Alfred A. Knopf, 1989.

Paley, Grace. *Collected Stories*. New York: Farrar, Straus and Giroux, 1994.

Perec, George. *Life: A User's Manual*. Translated by David Bellos. Boston: David R. Godine, 1987.

Perec, George. *A Void*. Translated by George Adair. London: Harvill, 1994.

Peretz, I. L. *The I. L. Peretz Reader*. Edited and with an introduction by Ruth R. Wisse. New York: Schocken Books, 1990.

Pinter, Harold. *Complete Works*. New York: Grove Weidenfeld, 1990.

Proust, Marcel. *In Search of Lost Time*. Translated by C. K. Scott Moncrieff. 4 vols. New York: Everyman's Library, 2001.

Richler, Mordecai. *The Apprenticeship of Duddy Kravitz*. New York: Little, Brown, 1959.

Roth, Philip. *Goodbye, Columbus*. Boston: Houghton Mifflin, 1959.

Roth, Philip. *Operation Shylock: A Confession*. New York: Simon & Schuster, 1993.

Schulz, Bruno. *Collected Works*. Edited by Jerzy Ficowski. London: Picador, 1998.

Scliar, Moacyr. *The Centaur in the Garden*. Translated by Margaret A. Neves. Introduction by Ilan Stavans. Madison: University of Wisconsin Press, 2003.

Scliar, Moacyr. *Collected Stories*. Translated by Eloah F. Giacomelli. Intoduction by Ilan Stavans. Albuquerque: University of New Mexico Press, 1999.

Shklovsky, Viktor. *Theory of Prose*. Translated by Benjamin Sher. Normal, IL: Dalkey Archive Press, 1990.

Singer, Isaac Bashevis. *Collected Stories*. 3 vols. Edited by Ilan Stavans. New York: Library of America, 2004.

Sontag, Susan. *Regarding the Pain of Others*. New York: Farrar, Straus and Giroux, 2003.

Sontag, Susan. *Sontag: Essays of the 1960s & 70s*. New York: Library of America, 2013.

Spiegelman, Art. *Maus: A Survivor's Tale*. New York: Pantheon, 1992.

Stavans, Ilan, ed. *The Oxford Book of Jewish Stories*. New York: Oxford University Press, 1998.

Stavans, Ilan, ed. *Oy, Caramba! An Anthology of Jewish Stories from Jewish Latin America*. Albuquerque: University of New Mexico Press, 2016.

Stavans, Ilan, ed. *The Schocken Book of Modern Sephardic Literature*. New York: Schocken Books, 2005.

Stavans, Ilan, with Josh Lambert, eds. *How Yiddish Changed America and How America Changed Yiddish*. Brooklyn: Restless Books, 2020.

Svevo, Italo. *Confessions of Zeno*. Translated by Beryl de Zoete. New York: Vintage, 1930.

Wiesel, Elie. *Night*. Translated by Marion Wiesel. New York: Hill & Wang, 2006.

Zangwill, Israel. *Children of the Ghetto: A Study of a Peculiar People*. Edited with an introduction by Meri-Jane Rochelson. Detroit: Wayne State University Press, 1998.

Secondary Sources

Asscher, Omri. *Reading Israel, Reading America: The Politics of Translation between Jews*. Stanford, CA: Stanford University Press, 2019.

Biale, David, David Assaf, Benjamin Brown, Uriel Gellman, Samuel C. Heilman, Murray Jay Rosman, Gad Sagiv, Marcin

Wodziński, and Arthur Green. *Hasidism: A New History*.
Princeton, NJ: Princeton University Press, 2018.

Bland, Kalman B. *The Artless Jew: Medieval and Modern Affirmations
and Denials of the Visual*. Princeton, NJ: Princeton University
Press, 2001.

Borges, Jorge Luis. *Labyrinths: Selected Stories & Other Writings*.
Edited by Donald A. Yates and James E. Irby. New York: New
Directions, 1964.

Castro, Américo. *The Structure of Spanish History*. Translated from
Spanish by Edmund L. King. Princeton, NJ: Princeton University
Press, 1954.

Dauber, Jeremy A. *Antonio's Devils: Writers of the Jewish
Enlightenment and the Birth of Modern Hebrew and Yiddish
Literature*. Stanford, CA: Stanford University Press, 2004.

Dauber, Jeremy A. *Jewish Comedy: A Serious History*. New York:
W. W. Norton, 2017.

Dynner, Glenn. *Men in Silk: The Hasidic Conquest of Polish Jewish
Society*. New York: Oxford University Press, 2006.

Eber, Irene. *Jews in China: Cultural Conversations, Changing
Perceptions*. Edited with an introduction by Katherine Hellerstein.
University Park: Pennsylvania University Press, 2019.

Fiedler, Leslie. *Fiedler on the Roof: Essays on Literature and Jewish
Identity*. Boston: David R. Godine, 1991.

Frakes, Jerold C. *The Emergence of Early Yiddish Literature: Cultural
Translation in Ashkenaz*. Bloomington: Indiana University
Press, 2017.

Gelbin, Cathy S., with Sander L. Gilman. *Cosmopolitanisms and the
Jews*. Ann Arbor: University of Michigan Press, 2017.

Gilman, Sander L. *Jewish Frontiers: Essays on Bodies, Histories, and
Identities*. New York: Palgrave Macmillan, 2003.

Gitlitz, David M. *Secrecy and Deceit: The Religion of the Crypto-Jews*.
Philadelphia: Jewish Publication Society of America, 1996.

Green, Arthur, with Ariel Evan Mayse, eds. *A New Hasidism: Roots*.
Lincoln: University of Nebraska Press, 2019.

Green, Arthur, with Ariel Evan Mayse, eds. *A New Hasidism:
Branches*. Lincoln: University of Nebraska Press, 2019.

Harshav, Benjamin. *The Meaning of Yiddish*. Stanford, CA: Stanford
University Press, 1990.

Hoberman, Michael. *A Hundred Acres of America: The Geography of
Jewish American Literary History*. New Brunswick, NJ: Rutgers
University Press, 2019.

Kahn, Lily. *The First Hebrew Shakespeare Translations: Isaac Edward Sakinson's Ithiel the Cushite of Venice and Ram and Jael*. Bilingual edition, with commentary. London: UCL Press, 2017.

Kahn, Lily. *A Grammar of the Eastern European Hasidic Hebrew Tale*. Leiden: Brill, 2015.

Katz, Jacob. *Out of the Ghetto: The Social Background of Jewish Emancipation, 1770–1870*. New York: Schocken Books, 1978.

Kellman, Steven G. *Nimble Tongues: Studies in Literary Translingualism*. West Lafayette, IN: Purdue University Press, 2020.

Kellman, Steven G. *The Translingual Imagination*. Lincoln: University of Nebraska Press, 2000.

Kirsch, Adam. *The People and the Books: 18 Classics of Jewish Literature*. New York: W. W. Norton, 2016.

Knott, Marie Louise, ed. *Hannah Arendt and Gerschom Scholem: Correspondence*. Translated by Anthony David. Chicago: University of Chicago Press, 2017.

Kronfeld, Chana. *The Full Severity of Compassion: The Poetry of Yehuda Amichai*. Stanford, CA: Stanford University Press, 2016.

Levinas, Emmanuel. *Nine Talmudic Readings*. Translated from French by Annette Aronowicz. Bloomington: Indiana University Press, 1990.

Matt, Daniel, trans. and com. *Zohar*. 12 vols. Stanford, CA: Stanford University Press, 2018.

Mendelson-Maoz, Adia. *Borders, Territories, and Ethics: Hebrew Literature in the Shadow of the Intifada*. West Lafayette, IN: Purdue University Press, 2018.

Mendelson-Maoz, Adia. *Multiculturalism in Israel: Literary Perspectives*. West Lafayette, IN: Purdue University Press, 2014.

Miccoli, Dario, ed. *Contemporary Sephardic and Mizrahi Literature: A Diaspora*. New York: Routledge, 2017.

Miller, Joshua J., with Anita Norich, eds. *Languages of Modern Jewish Cultures: Comparative Perspectives*. Ann Arbor: University of Michigan Press, 2016.

Miron, Dan. *The Animal in the Synagogue: Franz Kafka's Jewishness*. Translated from the Hebrew by Yitzhak Lewis. Lanham, MD: Lexington Books, 2019.

Miron, Dan. *From Continuity to Contiguity: Towards a New Jewish Literary Thinking*. Stanford, CA: Stanford University Press, 2010.

Norich, Anita. *Writing in Tongues: Translating Yiddish in the Twentieth Century*. Seattle: University of Washington Press, 2013.

Pinsker, Shachar. *Literary Passports: The Making of Modernist Hebrew Fiction in Europe*. Stanford, CA: Stanford University Press, 2011.

Pinsker, Shachar. *A Rich Brew: How Cafés Create Modern Jewish Culture*. New York: New York University Press, 2018.

Prager, Leonard. "Shakespeare in Yiddish," *Shakespeare Quarterly* 19, no. 2 (Spring 1968): 149–58.

Rosman, Moshe. *Founder of Hasidism: A Quest for the Historical Ba'al Shem Tov*. Los Angeles: University of California Press, 1996.

Roth, Cecil. *A History of the Marranos*. Philadelphia: Jewish Publication Society of America, 1932.

Shirer, William L. *The Rise and Fall of the Third Reich*. New York: Simon & Schuster, 1960.

Slucki, David, with Avinoam Pratt and Gabriel N. Finder, eds. *Laughter After: Humor and the Holocaust*. Detroit: Wayne State University Press, 2020.

Sokoloff, Naomi B., with Nancy E. Berg, eds. *What We Talk about When We Talk about Hebrew (and What It Means to Americans)*. Seattle: University of Washington Press, 2018.

Stavans, Ilan. *Borges, the Jew*. Albany: State University of New York Press, 2016.

Stavans, Ilan. *The Inveterate Dreamer: Essays and Conversations on Jewish Culture*. Lincoln: University of Nebraska Press, 2001.

Stavans, Ilan. *On Self-Translation: Meditations on Language*. Albany: State University of New York Press, 2018.

Stavans, Ilan. *Resurrecting Hebrew*. New York: Schocken Books, 2005.

Stavans, Ilan. *The Return of Carvajal: A Mystery*. University Park: Pennsylvania State University Press, 2019.

Stavans, Ilan. *Selected Translations: Poems, 2000–2020*. Pittsburgh, PA: University of Pittsburgh Press, 2021.

Stavans, Ilan. *The Seventh Heaven: Travels though Jewish Latin America*. Pittsburgh, PA: University of Pittsburgh Press, 2019.

Stavans, Ilan. *Singer's Typewriter and Mine: Reflections on Jewish Culture*. Lincoln: University of Nebraska Press, 2012.

Steiner, George. *After Babel: Aspects of Language and Translation*. Oxford: Oxford University Press, 1975.

Steiner, George. *Extraterritorial: Papers on Literature and the Language Revolution*. New York: Atheneum, 1971.

Steinsaltz, Adin, trans. and com. *The Talmud*. 22 vols. New York: Random House, 1989.

Weingrad, Michael. *American Hebrew Literature: Writing Jewish National Identity in the United States*. Foreword by Alan Mintz. Syracuse, NY: Syracuse University Press, 2011.

Weinreich, Max. *A History of the Yiddish Language*. 2 vols. New Haven, CT: Yale University Press, 2008.

Wisse, Ruth R. *The Modern Jewish Canon: A Journey through Language and Culture*. New York: Free Press, 2000.

Yerushalmi, Hayim Yosef. *Zakhor: Jewish History and Jewish Memory*. Seattle: University of Washington Press, 1982.

Yovel, Yirmiyahu. *The Other Within: The Marranos, Spilt Identity and Emerging Modernity*. Princeton, NJ: Princeton University Press, 2009.

Wills, Lawrence M., ed. *Ancient Jewish Novels: An Anthology*. Oxford: Oxford University Press, 2002.

Wirth-Nesher, Hana. *Call It English: The Languages of American Jewish Literature*. Princeton, NJ: Princeton University Press, 2009.

Wirth-Nesher, Hana, ed. *The Cambridge History of Jewish American Literature*. Cambridge: Cambridge University Press, 2016.

Index

Index

Index